FINANCIAL LEADERSHIP

for Nonprofit Executives

Guiding Your Organization to Long-term Success

Jeanne Bell and Elizabeth Schaffer
CompassPoint Nonprofit Services

FIELDSTONE
ALLIANCE

SAINT PAUL
MINNESOTA

We thank The David and Lucile Packard Foundation
for support of this publication.

Fieldstone Alliance is committed to strengthening the performance of the nonprofit sector. Through the synergy of its consulting, training, publishing, and research and demonstration projects, Fieldstone Alliance provides solutions to issues facing nonprofits, funders, and the communities they serve. Fieldstone Alliance was formerly Wilder Publishing and Wilder Consulting departments of the Amherst H. Wilder Foundation. If you would like more information about Fieldstone Alliance and our services, please contact us at 651-556-4500.

We hope you find this book useful! For information about other Fieldstone Alliance publications, contact:

Fieldstone Alliance Publishing Center
800-274-6024
www.FieldstoneAlliance.org

Edited by Vince Hyman
Text designed by Kirsten Nielsen
Cover designed by Rebecca Andrews

Manufactured in the United States of America
Third printing, April 2008

Library of Congress Cataloging-in-Publication Data

Bell, Jeanne, 1969-
   Financial leadership for nonprofit executives : guiding your organization to long-term success / by Jeanne Peters & Elizabeth Schaffer.
      p. cm.
   Includes bibliographical references.
   ISBN-13: 978-0-940069-44-2 (pbk.)
   ISBN-10: 0-940069-44-X (pbk.)
   1. Nonprofit organizations--Finance. I. Schaffer, Elizabeth, 1963- II. Title.
   HG4027.65.P48 2004
   658.15--dc22
                        2005001064

Financial Leadership for Nonprofit Executives is part of a series of works published by Fieldstone Alliance in partnership with CompassPoint Nonprofit Services of San Francisco, California. Together, we hope to strengthen the impact of nonprofit organizations and the people who work and volunteer for them as they strive to make our communities more vital and our democracy more just.

Other books in this series:

The Accidental Techie: Supporting, Managing, and Maximizing Your Nonprofit's Technology

The Best of the Board Café: Hands-on Solutions for Nonprofit Boards

About the Authors

JEANNE BELL PETERS is chief operating officer and a senior consultant at CompassPoint Nonprofit Services—a leading provider of training, consulting, and research to the nonprofit sector with offices in San Francisco and San Jose, California. Jeanne manages CompassPoint's finance practice, which includes finance workshops, forums and conferences, and consulting to nonprofit organizations in financial systems, planning, reporting, and business strategy. At CompassPoint, Jeanne also does organizational development consulting and has managed research on such topics as nonprofit staff retention and executive leadership. She serves on the Advisory Boards of the Institute for Nonprofit Organization Management (INOM) at the University of San Francisco and The Nonprofit Quarterly. She holds a master's in Nonprofit Administration from the University of San Francisco.

ELIZABETH (LIZ) SCHAFFER is a nonprofit management consultant and trainer. Liz served as the deputy director of a medium-sized AIDS organization and spent seven years at Citibank as a branch manager and personal banker. She is a very popular trainer at CompassPoint's workshops and conferences and has lectured in Nonprofit Financial Management at The Haas School of Business at UC Berkeley. In her consulting work, Liz works with twenty-five to thirty Bay Area nonprofit organizations each year. She helps clients enhance their decision-making ability by improving the quality of their financial data and analysis. Liz currently serves as a board member of Presidio Hill School and Equal Rights Advocates. She holds a master's in Nonprofit Administration from the University of San Francisco.

Contents

Figures

Acknowledgements

The authors gratefully acknowledge the contributions of our colleagues Tom Courtney, Consultant and Hydeh Ghaffari, CPA to the development of this book. Tom and Hydeh were very involved in early drafts and served as invaluable advisors as the concept for this book was taking shape.

We also want to thank Gary Page, Karen Schiller, and Brian Wilson, who have been our partners in training and consulting to Bay Area nonprofits. The five of us have developed training curricula together, debated best practices, and learned from each other how to be better at what we do. As such, their influences are evident throughout this book.

We want to thank CompassPoint's leadership—Executive Director Jan Masaoka, and Mike Allison, Director of Consulting and Research—for their guidance and support of this book. As with most projects of this scale, we went through many drafts (and budgets!), but their commitment did not waver. Jan's experience providing finance consulting to nonprofits made her an especially helpful reader and editorial advisor.

The official readers of our final draft manuscript provided us with extremely important feedback. We thank the following for volunteering their time and insight to make this a better book.

- Tom Courtney, Consultant
- Hilary Crosby, Crosby and Kaneda CPAs
- Scott Helgeson, Amherst H. Wilder Foundation
- Mark Jansen, CPA
- John Manzon-Santos, Executive Director, Asian and Pacific Islander Wellness Center
- Beverly McCarthy, President, Ashford Group, Inc.
- Gloria Nedved, CEO, Ripple Creek Business Solutions

- Aaron Nielsen, CPA, MMKR Public Accountants
- David White, Controller, Resources for Child Caring, Inc.
- Barry Zack, Executive Director, Centerforce

We would like to acknowledge Urvashi Vaid, Program Officer at the Ford Foundation, for her support of CompassPoint's finance efforts—including the first draft of what eventually became this book—between 2000 and 2002.

Finally, the authors are indebted to the many consulting clients and workshop participants who have taught us over the years what works in community-based organizations, and who inspire us every day with their commitment and leadership.

Introduction:
How to Use This Book

As consultants and trainers to nonprofit organizations of all mission types, we have learned first-hand that—as with most aspects of organizational effectiveness—financial strength is dependent on the leadership of a nonprofit's executive director. We have found that many people working and volunteering in the nonprofit sector expect executives to be well-versed in the program and fundraising arenas, but assume that finance is best left to a bookkeeper, a board treasurer, a Certified Public Accountant (CPA), or some combination thereof. On the contrary, our experience teaches us that financial health is so entwined with programming decisions and fundraising plans that the executive who avoids being informed about finance runs a real risk of jeopardizing an organization's future.

Still, becoming comfortable and confident with the financial aspect of nonprofit leadership can be challenging for executives. Thus, our goal in writing this book is to provide executives with a practical guide that recognizes that most of them will never be trained in accounting, nor is mastering financial jargon high on their list of priorities. Instead, nonprofit executives are concerned with protecting and growing the assets of their organizations and with accomplishing as much mission as possible with those resources. In the end, no nonprofit executive wants to leave an organization weaker than he or she found it.

CompassPoint's Finance Philosophy

CompassPoint Nonprofit Services is a nonprofit organization serving other nonprofits through workshops, conferences, consulting, and publications. Our perspective on finance is shaped by our commitment to community-based organizations of all types—as well as our belief in their numerous assets and pivotal role in society. We don't think nonprofits are broken and in need of fixing; instead we recognize the complexity of issues nonprofit leaders have to embrace, and in this book we present a framework for understanding the financial aspect of leadership. We do so with our eyes on the mission prize; that is, we see finance as a way to understand and better plan for programmatic success. Finance is not an end in itself, but a necessary lens through which nonprofit leaders can look at their activities and organizational sustainability.

Having said this, we also believe that nonprofit leaders have to face up to the accountability mandate—not just from the IRS or legislators—but from the people their organizations intend to benefit. In part, this means building individual and organizational capacity to follow the rules of nonprofit accounting and establishing a culture of transparency around money. Small and midsized organizations that identify themselves as "grassroots" are not exempt from this mandate. On the contrary, our opinion is that financial transparency is directly in line with the values of being relevant, responsive, and committed to a broad range of social change.

Who This Book Is For

We have written this book for executive directors of 501(c)(3) public charities. We also think that the executive director's key partners in financial leadership—board members, finance staff, and other senior management team members—will benefit from this book's approach. The orientation of the book is to *consumers* of financial information rather than *producers*. In other words, the book's objective is not to teach the reader transactional accounting, but rather to help him or her use financial information in decision-making. Finally, because our work is typically with nonprofit organizations in the $500,000 to $10,000,000 budget range, the book's tone and examples respond to the issues facing leaders of organizations of this size.

How to Use This Book

This book is organized around a financial leadership model. The model has four components: ensure accuracy, assess, plan, and communicate. Chapter 1 defines financial leadership, while Chapters 2 through 5 explain the four components of the model. Figure 1 represents the Financial Leadership Model; you will find components of this image throughout the book to remind you of where you are in the process.

Figure 1. Financial Leadership Model

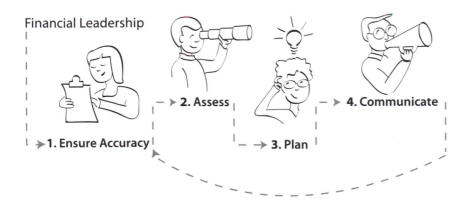

Before you can dive into assessing, planning for, and communicating the financial health of your organization, you need to be both familiar with financial leadership principles and confident that the financial data you are consuming is credible. Therefore, we encourage you to read Chapters 1 and 2 before you read further.

Case Study

This book includes a recurring case study that is designed to illustrate the key learning objectives. All of the examples and sample financial statements throughout the book are for a fictional organization called Domestic Violence Intervention & Prevention, or DV for short. We intend the case study to have two benefits: first, it will help you understand the book's concepts by providing life-like examples; and second, it may provide you with sample statements and formats that you can use to improve your own organization's financial reporting.

To orient you to the case study, here is some background information about Domestic Violence Intervention & Prevention. The organization employs nineteen staff members and has an annual budget of $1.5 million. Founded over ten years ago, DV began as a safe house for survivors of domestic violence. With the help of key individuals in the private sector and the support of the city, DV has flourished and expanded its services to include:

- A shelter that can accommodate twenty women and ten children
- Five support groups each week for women and children living with or leaving batterers

Elena Rodriguez, DV's executive director, came to the organization as its first shelter manager eight years ago. She has been the executive director for two

---

Case Study:
Domestic Violence Intervention & Prevention

We use a fictional case study throughout this book to illustrate key points. Here are the key attributes of the case study, in a nutshell:

- Ten years in existence
- Executive director, Elena Rodriguez
- Nineteen staff
- $1.5 million budget

Services include shelter for twenty women and ten children, and five support groups per week.

years now. In the past few months, she and DV's board of directors have faced several financial challenges; they are eager to learn more about DV's financial condition and plan effectively for its future.

Some totals in the sample financial statements may be off by one digit due to rounding in the Excel document. You can download the entire Excel document that includes most of the figures found in this book, by visiting the URLs listed below.

Red/Yellow/Green Evaluation Tool

We have created an evaluation tool that will help you determine where your organization is now relative to the component of financial leadership covered in each chapter. We use this evaluation tool in our work with community-based nonprofits. In the evaluation process, we score each measured attribute as being red, yellow, or green. The "red" items are below standard and require immediate attention; "yellow" items are widely practiced though not generally ideal; and "green" items are considered best practice. An organization can function quite well with a mix of "green" and "yellow" attributes, while an organization with a majority of "red" attributes is likely feeling the strain of financial underperformance and the disengagement of board and management from the organization's financial condition. Over time, as you and your partners on the board and staff move the organization toward "green" in each of these areas, you will create an environment in which financial leadership can flourish.

The tool also includes space for your comments about each item measured as well as for your action plan to address it. At the end of each chapter of the book, you will see how Elena, DV's executive director, responds to the Red/Yellow/Green Evaluation Tool. This is intended to give you a life-like example of how the evaluation is completed. You can find a complete, blank evaluation for photocopying in Appendix B. Or you can download a copy at the following URLs:

http://www.FieldstoneAlliance.org/worksheets   (Code: W44XfL05)

http://www.compasspoint.org

A couple of additional points about the evaluation tool: First, remember that organizational lifecycle stage—where an organization is on the continuum from young start-up to institutional maturity—is often a factor in how close to best practice it is. More mature organizations have had more time and resources to invest in infrastructure (though not all do unfortunately). Secondly,

Red = items are below standard and require immediate attention

Yellow = items are widely practiced though not generally ideal

Green = items are considered best practice

in the vast majority of cases, the reasons for "red" findings in the evaluation of a community-based nonprofit have nothing to do with fraud or flagrant disregard for accountability; on the contrary, they usually are the result of a lack of skills or knowledge among finance staff, the leadership team, and the board of directors. Your objective in conducting the evaluation is not to blame current or former staff and board, but to surface the priority areas for attention from you and your financial leadership partners.

Further Resources

Finally, there are some important resources at the back of this book. You will find definitions of all underlined words in Appendix A, Key Terms. (Note: a key term is underlined only on its first appearance in the book.) While Chapters 2 through 5 each end with a portion of the Red/Yellow/Green Evaluation Tool, a complete version for use at your organization can be found in Appendix B. Appendix C is an annotated list of periodicals, books, and web sites that we think are helpful to financial leaders.

1. Defining Financial Leadership

As the nonprofit sector has grown and matured over the last thirty years, the prevailing attitudes about money of its leaders, donors, and institutional funders have evolved. Early on, the assumption was that nonprofits were fundamentally different from businesses. During the 1960s, '70s, and '80s, when hundreds of thousands of community-based arts, advocacy, health, and social service nonprofits were founded, there was very little pressure on nonprofit leaders to speak in financial terms; instead, the nearly exclusive focus was on mission, programs and activities, and fundraising success. By the end of the 1990s, however, the notion of running a nonprofit more like a for-profit business had emerged. This was largely driven by the dramatic changes in the broader economy, philanthropy's growing interest in measuring effectiveness, and publicity around a handful of financial scandals.

Looking to the for-profit sector, nonprofits—or at least their funders and external stakeholders—began adopting concepts such as efficiency and entrepreneurialism. If you were working in the sector during this period, you'll remember that nonprofits began adapting to this new climate by using words like "leverage" and "social return on investment" more than they ever had before. Certainly not all of the practices behind these catchphrases were institutionalized by most small and midsized nonprofits, but it was nonetheless clear that the public's expectations of nonprofit leaders had shifted in the direction of business. As our implicit exemption from financial rigor evaporated, nonprofits' *dual* bottom line—mission *and* money—came into focus. We think that the sector is entering a third phase where those working and investing in it will recognize that the leaders of our community-based nonprofits are not running anti-businesses; nor are they running for-profit businesses in nonprofit disguise. *They are running nonprofit businesses.*

A *nonprofit business* is an organization driven by its community objectives and organized to obtain and manage the financial resources necessary to accomplish those objectives.

When mission perpetually (and heavily) outweighs money, it may be that key people inside the organization are stuck in the "nonprofits can't make money" mind-set.

Mission or Money?

What is a nonprofit business? A *nonprofit business* is an organization driven by its community objectives *and* organized to obtain and manage the financial resources necessary to accomplish those objectives. If we think of this as a balancing act with mission and money on either side, a nonprofit business has achieved the critical balance between the two.

In a nonprofit business, money is not a "necessary evil" or something that should never be mentioned in the same hallowed breath as mission. Rather, leaders in a nonprofit business grapple openly with how to make limited resources go as far as possible for their constituencies.

There are a number of organizational attributes that can prevent a nonprofit organization from achieving this elusive balance. If the organization leans too heavily toward mission, three problems typically emerge: 1) the organization functions in a state of continual financial crisis; 2) the organization under-invests in infrastructure, jeopardizing its future; and/or 3) the organization does not include financial performance in its evaluation of programmatic success. Let's look at each of these problems.

When mission perpetually (and heavily) outweighs money, it may be that key people inside the organization are stuck in the "nonprofits can't make money" mind-set. Some in the nonprofit sector call this the "culture of scarcity." Symptoms of the culture of scarcity may include underpaying key staff, delaying payments to vendors, or even taking risks with mandatory payroll tax withholdings. In organizations where this is the culture around money, financial crisis is the norm. In subtle or not-so-subtle ways, the never-ending crisis is held up as symbolizing that the organization has not "sold out." But the fact is, extended financial crisis is exhausting. It depletes the energy and creativity it takes to accomplish ambitious programming.

Another characteristic of nonprofits that lean too heavily toward mission is underinvestment in infrastructure. Again, people inside the organization—at times with collusion from donors and institutional funders—are unwilling to direct sufficient financial resources toward infrastructure such as accounting, auditing, and financial management training to staff and board. They reason that those financial resources could be helping additional people to find jobs or learn the impacts of global warming, or whatever the mission may be. What's lost in this argument is that in the long run, only those nonprofit businesses that do a good job of obtaining and managing money will thrive (not merely survive) long enough to have the deepest community impacts.

Finally, a third trait of nonprofits that lean too heavily toward mission is their tendency to subsidize activities that are not performing financially. In many cases this subsidy is unwitting because the organization's leaders do not have financial reporting of sufficient quality to determine which of their activities generate surplus funds and which deplete them. This is not to suggest that nonprofits should never maintain activities that are unable to cover their costs; indeed most nonprofit businesses will do this and do it gladly. Instead the concern here is that financial performance is not included in the evaluation of activities—only mission alignment is considered. In this case, organizations do not challenge themselves to attract additional funding, contain costs, or even reassess their programming, because they are unaccustomed or unwilling to consider "market forces" in their organizational planning.

Just as undesirable is an organization weighed down by an overemphasis on money to the detriment of mission accomplishment.

Just as undesirable is an overemphasis on money to the detriment of mission accomplishment.

In some nonprofits, this takes the form of pursuing funding such as foundation grants and government contracts regardless of their mission alignment—"chasing the money," it's often called. A money-over-mission mind-set may stem from (or be exacerbated by) a board of directors made up largely of for-profit business people. Without proper orientation and board education, these leaders may bring their "single bottom line" thinking to bear without enough nonprofit business nuances. When money is the only lens through which activities are evaluated, nonprofits become afraid to invest in unfunded program start-up (the nonprofit equivalent of the for-profit sector's research and development) or to raise funds to subsidize essential programs that cannot be self-sufficient.

The premise of this book is that effective nonprofit businesses—those that strike the balance between mission and money—are the result of *financial leadership*. Though a nonprofit business actually benefits from a number of people on board and staff with financial leadership traits, the executive director must play the role of financial leader in a nonprofit business. The executive director is the financial leader because she or he is the person primarily responsible for the health and performance of the organization overall. Just as in the program and fundraising arenas, the executive director must have a vision of where the organization is heading financially and how it will get there.

Financial Leadership

Financial leadership is ensuring that decision makers have *timely and accurate* financial data; using financial data to *assess* the financial condition of your activities and nonprofit business overall; *planning* around a set of meaningful financial goals; and *communicating* progress on these goals to your staff, board, and external stakeholders. It is not being a trained accountant, or having an MBA, or even having run a for-profit business in another lifetime. While none of those things can hurt, they are not requirements of exercising financial leadership.

Assessment, planning, and communication—these familiar leadership skills are the same skills you would use to develop a new community-based program, or even to achieve a personal goal such as physical fitness or getting out of debt. We don't mean to downplay the unique vocabulary or concepts of nonprofit finance, but we do want to suggest that financial leadership is part of organizational leadership. As such, it requires the same cohort of skills as programmatic or fundraising leadership.

Figure 2. Financial Leadership Model

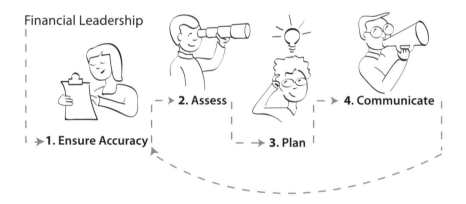

The Financial Leadership Model's elements are both interdependent and cyclical. Without accurate financial data, one cannot assess financial health. Without quality assessment, one cannot set meaningful goals. Without shared goals, communicating about progress is flat and unengaging, and so on. Moreover, financial leadership is not required once a year (for instance, solely during the annual budgeting process), but all year long, every year. Decisions as varied as whether to begin or end a program, to hire your first development director, or to enter into a partnership with another nonprofit organization, if made effectively, draw on the skills presented in this model. Chapters 2 through 5 of this book provide full discussion of each element of financial leadership.

Financial leadership is

1. Ensuring that decision makers have timely and accurate financial data. (This sets the groundwork for the cycle of assessment, planning, and communication.)

2. Using financial data to assess the financial condition of your activities and nonprofit business overall.

3. Planning around a set of meaningful financial goals.

4. Communicating progress on these goals to your staff, board, and external stakeholders.

Five Leadership Principles

If it is time to bring mission and money into balance at your nonprofit and you want to work intentionally on developing your own financial leadership skills, there are five foundational principles to consider:

1. Move beyond mission-versus-money thinking.
2. Cultivate financial leadership on both staff and board.
3. View the nonprofit business as an interdependent set of programs and activities.
4. Recognize the relationship between strong infrastructure and strong programs.
5. Set a tone of financial accountability and transparency.

As you review each principle, take some time to assess where you have been and where you are now as a leader in each of these areas. These five principles will be essential to putting the rest of the book's recommendations into practice.

1. Move beyond mission-versus-money thinking

By definition, a nonprofit business has moved beyond the view of mission and money as antithetical. As the financial leader, you want to convey to staff and board that you hold *both* a deep passion for the mission of your organization and pragmatism about how to finance its work. Indicators that you have led the organization to this stance include:

- You regularly raise the financial implications of ideas generated in strategic and program planning sessions.
- You hold management meetings in which the organization's financial health is a standing agenda item.
- You do not delegate all discussions and updates on financial health to a finance staff person.

In these instances, staff and board get the clear message that you are unwilling to focus on mission to the exclusion of money. Since many people are uncomfortable talking about money, if you don't do it openly and regularly, others may be happy to follow your lead and a culture of mission versus money—rather than mission *and* money—will take root.

2. Cultivate financial leadership on both staff and board

An effective financial leader likes company. This is not because you can find that perfect finance manager or board treasurer who will allow you to never have to think about finance again. (Remember, you are the financial leader.) On the contrary, you need people to complement your own skills and experience. The most obvious example of this is someone to do the accounting, but there are other financial skill sets you'll need too. For instance, it is invaluable to have a finance professional or a Certified Public Accountant (CPA) on your board of directors. This way you ensure that at least one of your directors has a full understanding of accounting principles and will be informed of major changes in accounting regulations; senior nonprofit finance staff or CPAs with nonprofit practices are even more valuable because they understand nonprofit businesses. You can also seek program staff that has had experience in program budgeting or creating grant proposal budgets. And if you have inexperienced staff and board, it is crucial that you invest in their financial education through workshops, books, online learning, and conferences. As the financial leader, one of your essential roles is to recruit and mentor managers and board members who will add to the creativity and sophistication of the financial dialogue at the organization.

3. View the nonprofit business as an interdependent set of programs and activities

Perhaps the biggest financial leadership decision an executive makes—with significant input and direction from the board, staff, and community—is how to use the financial resources of the organization to accomplish the mission. Initially, a nonprofit business may consist of one core program in addition to its fundraising and administrative activities. Usually as an organization matures, it engages in several core programs in pursuit of its mission. For instance, our case study organization, DV, has both a shelter for battered women and support groups for women leaving batterers. As the financial leader, you want to take a holistic view of your portfolio of activities because they are financially interdependent. In the case of DV, the support groups are largely funded by foundation grants, which also make a contribution to the administrative activity; the shelter is funded by a government contract and the special events the organization's fundraising activity conducts each year, and so on. As the leader, you are responsible for the financial health of the individual activities as well as the whole.

This identification of core competencies and core activities takes time. Many nonprofit organizations are created through the intense enthusiasm of their founder and volunteers. At this early stage, everyone does everything—and exactly what they're doing is less defined. But as an organization develops, primary activities come into focus and the need to understand them as distinct for the purposes of clear planning and communication soon follows. In human service organizations like DV, it is very common in the early stages of development to equate major funding sources with major program areas, but this always becomes problematic eventually. Core programs stay with an organization, while individual funding sources come and go.

4. Recognize the relationship between strong infrastructure and strong programs

This principle builds on the notion of a nonprofit business as a set of interdependent activities. In a nonprofit business, your investment in administration (such as finance and board development) and fundraising is an investment in the essential infrastructure of your organization. These non-program activities have a direct effect on the success of your programs. For instance, a weak board of directors will mean insufficient strategic thinking about your organization's potential; a disorganized fundraising effort will leave your valuable programs vulnerable to funding cuts. Of course the scale of your infrastructure will depend on the size of your nonprofit business; we are not advocating an excessive investment here. But at any scale, an appropriate finance function means among other things the ability to manage your contributed funds in compliance with nonprofit accounting standards; to maintain relationships with the vendors who provide you with the materials you need to accomplish your work; and to make payroll so that your valuable employees can continue to work for you. As the financial leader, you want to establish a culture within both staff and board that values infrastructure and invests in it appropriately and unapologetically.

Establish a culture within both staff and board that values infrastructure and invests in it appropriately and unapologetically.

5. Set a tone of financial accountability and transparency

The words "accountability" and "transparency" are currently everywhere in both the for-profit and nonprofit sectors. High-profile scandals in both arenas have made accountability the topic of countless speeches, op-eds, conference sessions, and even legislation. But when they are eventually replaced by new buzzwords, accountability and transparency will still be essential to nonprofit success because they generate credibility and confidence among donors, who are the lifeblood of a nonprofit business. It is the executive director—in partnership with the board of directors—who must set this tone. In setting a tone of accountability, the executive articulates frequently—both internally and externally—that the organization is financially accountable to its staff, board, donors and funders, clients and constituents, the IRS, and so on. As the leader, if you compromise on this point, the people around you will likely follow suit. If you believe that you are financially accountable to these multiple constituencies, you will insist that the organization share financial information with them. This will take a myriad of forms, from providing accurate, meaningful financial statements to staff and board, to producing an annual report to the community, to posting your IRS Form 990 on your web site. As donors and institutional funders become savvier about evaluating nonprofit businesses, those who have nothing to hide will be positioned far more strongly than those who keep financial information hidden from public view.

Evaluate Your Financial Leadership

To help you consider your personal financial leadership strengths and areas for improvement at this juncture, review Figure 3, Financial Leadership Self-Evaluation on pages 16–17. These are questions to help you assess the extent to which you are currently working in alignment with the five foundational principles described in this chapter. This tool is not comprehensive in nature; instead the statements are intended to help you consider aspects of your leadership style that may be unconscious, but nevertheless help to establish a particular culture around money at your organization. Elena's answers, comments, and action steps are included here to give you a sense of how to think about these questions and their implications. A blank version is included in Appendix B.

Notice that none of the statements in Figure 3—or the five foundational principles upon which they are based—involves uniquely financial terms or concepts. Yes, some of those terms and concepts appear in the chapters that follow, but the critical point at this juncture is that to exercise financial leadership, a nonprofit business draws on general leadership skills: understanding the nature of the business you are running, surrounding yourself with the right people, and communicating and eliciting feedback from your stakeholders. In other words, even if you were a trained nonprofit accountant, if you didn't have these other skills you couldn't exercise financial leadership. Indeed, we are guessing that you already have many of the skills it takes to be a financial leader; the rest of this book aims to provide you with the specific language and processes to do it confidently.

Summary

Executive directors are the financial leaders of nonprofit organizations. Though they do not manage the day-to-day financial transactions of their organizations, the quality of decisions they make as leaders very much depends on their ability to assess, plan for, and communicate the financial condition of their organizations. In our experience, executives who never cultivate this element of leadership are less effective at guiding their organizations to financial and programmatic sustainability.

Chapter 1 argued for a mission-money balance in nonprofit organizational culture and outlined the five foundational principles of effective financial leadership. Understanding those principles is important, but not enough. Finance involves numbers, and you can't lead without good numbers reflecting your organization's financial situation. Chapter 2 will explore the systems you need to have in place so that you can get reliable data.

Figure 3.   Financial Leadership Self-Evaluation

Category	Getting Started	A Work in Progress	Key Competency	Comments	Action Plan
Personal Leadership	I do not yet consider myself the financial leader of this organization.	I am trying to consider myself the financial leader of this organization.	I absolutely consider myself the financial leader of this organization.	I do now consider myself the financial leader of DV, but I wasn't really ready for this until recently.	Continue to role-model financial leadership; seek feedback from my management team and board.
Priorities	The financial health of this organization is not yet one of my top priorities.	The financial health of this organization is becoming one of my top priorities.	The financial health of this organization is absolutely one of my top priorities.	As a program person, I tend to focus on the clients versus the organization's money.	Ask for help from my finance manager and board treasurer; seek feedback.
Information Sharing	I do not yet share financial information with staff, and I regularly raise both programmatic and financial issues for consideration at our meetings.	I am working on sharing financial information with staff, and I regularly raise both programmatic and financial issues for consideration at our meetings.	I absolutely share financial information with staff, and I regularly raise both programmatic and financial issues for consideration at our meetings.	I do raise financial matters in our meetings, but it's hard to get folks focused. I think we have a way to go in creating meaningful financial reports for both board and staff.	Work with finance manager to design meaningful reports for both staff and board.
Board of Directors	I do not yet ensure that my board of directors discusses our financial situation at every board meeting.	I am working toward ensuring that my board of directors discusses our financial situation at every board meeting.	I ensure that my board of directors discusses our financial situation at every board meeting.	The board demands that I discuss our financial situation at every board meeting.	Work with board members to refine key financial questions and ensure available data.
Teamwork	I have not yet surrounded myself with enough financially savvy staff, consultants, and board members to feel confident that we have the necessary financial guidance for our organization.	I am trying to surround myself with enough financially savvy staff, consultants, and board members to feel confident that we have the necessary financial guidance for our organization.	I absolutely have surrounded myself with enough financially savvy staff, consultants, and board members to feel confident that we have the necessary financial guidance for our organization.	I have a great finance manager and board treasurer. Sometimes they find it hard to communicate with the program folks and I need to play translator. We're working on this.	Work one-on-one with program staff to develop finance skills.
Financial Knowledge	Without consulting financial statements or budgets, I cannot yet readily name our core programs and offer a good estimate of how much we'll spend on each this year.	Without consulting financial statements or budgets, I can almost name our core programs and offer a good estimate of how much we'll spend on each this year.	Without consulting financial statements or budgets, I can readily name our core programs and offer a good estimate of how much we'll spend on each this year.	We have two programs: a shelter for victims of domestic violence ($850k) and support groups for women who are currently victims or at risk of violence ($400k).	Ensure that program staff are equally fluent with program budget as with their annual program plan.

Figure 3. Financial Leadership Self-Evaluation continued

Category	Getting Started	A Work in Progress	Key Competency	Comments	Action Plan
Financial Performance	I do not yet know which of our core activities generate surpluses and which lose money.	I almost have a handle on which of our core activities generate surpluses and which lose money.	I absolutely know which of our core activities generate surpluses and which lose money.	For the longest time, we thought that our funding sources covered the costs associated with our key programs. We're learning this isn't entirely true.	Continue to analyze our cost allocation structure.
Investment in Infrastructure	I do not yet feel as comfortable investing the organization's resources in a great bookkeeper as I do in a great program staff person.	I feel almost as comfortable investing the organization's resources in a great bookkeeper as I do in a great program staff person.	I absolutely feel as comfortable investing the organization's resources in a great bookkeeper as I do in a great program staff person.	I came to this organization as the manager of the shelter, and I have seen firsthand what our clients go through. I'm learning that the finance office is critical to our ability to deliver services—but it's new for me!	Ask for help from my finance manager and board treasurer; seek feedback.
Funder Accountability	I am not yet ready to share our financial data with our funders and stakeholders.	I am almost ready to help our funders and stakeholders understand how we use financial resources to accomplish our mission.	I absolutely want our funders and stakeholders to understand how we use financial resources to accomplish our mission.	As I come to understand that our funders do not provide sufficient resources to cover our core programs, I am eager to share this information with them.	Schedule face-to-face meetings with key funders.
Establish a Culture of Transparency around Money	The staff and board do not yet know for sure that I value financial transparency.	The staff and board are beginning to understand that I value financial transparency.	The staff and board absolutely know for sure that I value financial transparency.	I have an open door and open "books" policy. While anyone can ask to see information at any time, some of our data is not clear, so it doesn't always answer all of the questions.	Keep the door open!

2. Getting Financial Data You Can Trust

As executive director and financial leader, your primary interest is in the programmatic and financial *performance* of your nonprofit business activities. But, the leadership model that we outlined in Chapter 1 requires that appropriate financial *processes* be in place. To exercise your assessment, planning, and communication leadership roles, you need accurate financial data, and you need it in a format you can understand. Clearly, inaccurate data would cause you to set potentially unrealistic goals and would also undermine your ability to communicate progress. But ensuring that the appropriate processes are in place can be a challenge for an executive who does not have a background in finance. Executives often ask us, "How am I supposed to know if my finance person knows what he or she is doing when I don't speak the language of accounting?" People sometimes compare this feeling to the vulnerability most of us feel when we take a car to a mechanic. Who are we to argue with a mechanic's $1,500 diagnosis when we don't know the difference between a carburetor and an alternator?

Despite these challenges, the first step toward exercising financial leadership has to be determining whether or not the financial information you have is credible. There are three key factors to consider here: staffing, accounting practices, and the accounting system.

Staffing

Let's start with staffing. You need to be confident that you have adequate financial staffing before you put your full trust in the financial statements being provided to you. Whether your financial people are employees, contract bookkeepers, or consulting CPAs, the most important question you have to answer is, "Do they understand and have experience with *nonprofit* accounting?" For instance, the issue of restricted contributions and how to present

In order to have confidence in the accuracy of your financial statements, you need to feel assured that the producers of the statements are not undertrained, overworked, or inappropriately isolated.

them on financial statements is unique to nonprofit businesses. You cannot assume that a board volunteer from the for-profit world—or even a trained bookkeeper—is familiar with this and other nonprofit-specific concepts. Carefully check resumes and references to determine that your financial staff is competent in nonprofit finance. If, for financial or other reasons, you choose staff that lack nonprofit experience, it is your responsibility as the financial leader of the organization to invest in training for them.

The second consideration in staffing is whether you have the right number of people. Even the best-trained nonprofit accountant cannot keep up when the volume of work is too high for one person. Having sufficient staffing—or a combination of staff and outside expertise—is also important for maintaining internal controls. If just one person in your organization receives funds, deposits funds, enters bills, issues checks, and does the monthly bank account reconciliation, you can see how that opens the door to possible undetected fraud. In small organizations with few staff, maintaining internal controls can be especially challenging. You will have to involve board members and other staff as appropriate to adequately segregate key financial duties and insert opportunities for checks and balances.[1]

Another thing to keep in mind about staffing is that your organization may not need a full-time senior finance manager. Perhaps your volume of finance work does not warrant it, but as the leader you do need access to a strategic financial partner. In this case, consider hiring somebody at half-time or even less, or using an independent contractor to add expertise and another pair of eyes for internal controls. However you staff your finance function, to have confidence in the accuracy of your financial statements, you need to feel assured that the producers of the statements are not undertrained, overworked, or inappropriately isolated.

We have found it helpful to consider finance staffing in three categories: strategic, operational, and transactional. Figure 4, Finance Functions, Specific Tasks, and Qualifications, page 21, defines these categories and provides examples of the tasks and qualifications for each category.

The size and complexity of your organization will determine how you accomplish each of these categories of work using a combination of board and volunteers, staff, or consultants and contractors. At DV (which you will recall has a budget of $1.5 million and a staff of nineteen), the accounting office has two staff: Frida, a full-time director of finance and administration, and Albert, a half-time accounting manager. Frida focuses on the strategic and operational aspects of both finance and human resources; Albert handles all of the transactional tasks.

---

[1] For guidance on establishing internal controls, see Chapters 8 and 9 of *Bookkeeping Basics: What Every Nonprofit Bookkeeper Needs to Know*, by Debra Ruegg and Lisa M. Venkatrathnam, published in 2003 by Fieldstone Alliance.

Figure 4. Finance Functions, Specific Tasks, and Qualifications

Finance Functions	Specific Tasks	Qualifications
Strategic *Perform the planning and oversight role for the finance department; guide accounting activities as needed*	• Conduct general financial planning and provide oversight • Develop a cost allocation framework • Analyze financial reports on a monthly basis and submit reports to the board and executive director on a monthly basis • Monitor financial activities; conduct a periodic comparison to the budget • Lead the annual budgeting process • Serve as the main point of contact with the auditor	• Strong analytical skills • Excellent communication skills • Exposure to nonprofit financial statement analysis • Program planning and nonprofit budgeting
Operational *Pay bills, invoice contracts, follow up on accounts receivable, prepare bank deposits, process payroll, and perform other accounting duties as assigned*	• Prepare A/P, A/R, and 1099 forms • Make cash disbursements • Complete contract invoicing (including the preparation of monthly reports to funders) • Report hours by program to the payroll-processing agency • Perform journal entries • Assist with budget and financial statement preparation • Monitor cash flow • Allocate all expenses (code checks) to the appropriate programs and grants based on the established cost allocation methodology • Respond to ad hoc analytic requests from the finance director	• Strong skills in Microsoft Excel • Strong nonprofit accounting experience (A/R, A/P), and experience in accounting for restricted grants • Experience in preparing financial statements from an accounting software system • Quick, accurate worker
Transactional *Support the accounting function by performing clerical and administrative tasks*	• Write checks once they are coded • Distribute financial statements to program managers • Photocopy checks, invoices, and other documents as required, and maintain check and invoice files • Make bank deposits • Maintain grant binders (obtain grant agreements, copies of monthly reports, and other necessary grant documentation) • Maintain personnel files • Collect time sheets	• Exposure to basic accounting principles • Strong attention to detail

In addition to accounting functions, you will want to evaluate the staffing involved in managing grants and contracts if you receive them. While accounting staff often handle these tasks, they require a different skill set than that required for traditional accounting. The person or people financially tracking your grants and contracts must have an understanding of the donors' intent and related accounting rules, knowledge of OMB A-133 (for government contracts), experience with monitoring budgets and forecasting expenses, and the ability to communicate effectively with development and program staff. An executive director must carefully assess the skills of his or her staffing here, obtaining training for staff as needed, because this area of nonprofit finance can expose the organization to risk (as in the case of misspent restricted grants or contracts).

If you get an annual audit of your financial statements, ask your auditor what his or her impressions are of your finance staff's capacity. While they are on-site at your organization, the auditors should get a good feel for how well prepared your staff were for the audit, how often your staff did not understand or implement key accounting principles, and whether staff are improving from year to year. Another option is hiring an outside financial consultant to do a staffing assessment. In short, rather than living with that nagging feeling that things are not running the way they should be, use the expert advice around you to help assess whether or not you have adequately trained staff.

Producers of financial data who are inflexible or indifferent to the needs of their consumers can represent a huge roadblock on your path to strengthening financial leadership in your organization.

Finally, as your organization's leader, you are looking for finance staff that share your attitude that finance is an essential part of infrastructure and that it should be done in the spirit of supporting programs and mission. The quality of financial information you receive will suffer if the people preparing it aren't interested in your organization's work. It will suffer if they are not responsive to your needs to evaluate the financial performance of your activities. Producers of financial data who are inflexible or indifferent to the needs of their consumers can represent a huge roadblock on your path to strengthening financial leadership in your organization. Too many nonprofit leaders feel held hostage by unresponsive finance staff because they are insecure about their own finance knowledge or afraid they won't find an adequate replacement. We encourage you to remember that you are the financial leader, which means you are entitled to ask questions and receive helpful answers from the people you hire to support you in that role.

Accounting Practices

Just as appropriate staffing is a requirement for accurate financial data, so too is implementation of certain accounting practices. Though you are not an accountant, your awareness and understanding of several key accounting practices will allow you to get a good sense for how accurate and well presented your financial data is. Here, we'll define six accounting practices that you need to ensure are in place before you rely on the financial statements provided to you. (Remember, you can find full definitions of any underlined word or concept in Appendix A, Key Terms.) The six practices are:

1. Treatment of restricted contributions
2. Functional classification of expenses
3. Employee time tracking
4. Allocation of common costs
5. Accrual basis accounting
6. Capitalization and depreciation

1. Treatment of restricted contributions

The first accounting practice you'll need to confirm is the presentation of restricted contributions on your financial statements. As you know, many contributors to nonprofit organizations place a programmatic and/or time restriction on how their contributions may be used. For instance, DV has a restricted foundation grant that can only be spent on providing support groups for clients. It is a leadership function—and a key element of nonprofit accountability—to ensure that restricted contributions are spent according to their donors' intent. If your financial statements do not convey that funds you have on hand carry a restriction, you might inadvertently spend the funds elsewhere and be unable to perform the grant or contract deliverables in the time frame required.

Contributions have one of three levels of restriction. <u>Unrestricted contributions</u> can be spent on any activities and in any time period the recipient organization chooses. <u>Temporarily restricted contributions</u> have to be spent on specific activities and/or in a particular time period as stipulated by the contributor. <u>Permanently restricted contributions</u> are to be held in perpetuity, usually as an <u>endowment</u>. Typically, when nonprofit staff talk about "restricted grants," they are referring to temporarily restricted contributions from foundations or major donors. Once a nonprofit organization receives a temporarily restricted contribution, it has to monitor expenses according to the budget ap-

> **Six Key Accounting Practices for Nonprofits**
>
> 1. Treatment of restricted contributions
> 2. Functional classification of expenses
> 3. Employee time tracking
> 4. Allocation of common costs
> 5. Accrual basis accounting
> 6. Capitalization and depreciation

Permanently restricted funds   Temporarily restricted funds

Unrestricted funds

Because net assets are where readers of financial statements look to determine the reserve of the organization, it is critical that they not blend unrestricted and restricted amounts in the presentation.

proved by the donor. As the nonprofit spends money according to that budget, it is <u>releasing funds from restriction</u>. In other words, it is the act of doing the promised work that allows a nonprofit to consider the funds unrestricted and available to cover expenses.

Figure 5, page 25, is DV's <u>Statement of Activities</u>, which describes its income and expenses for the fiscal year to date. (This is the nonprofit version of a Profit and Loss Statement or "P&L.") On it, you'll find a column dedicated to temporarily restricted funds—those contributions with a time and/or programmatic restriction. You also see a column dedicated to permanently restricted contributions—those funds for which the principle must be held in perpetuity. This columnar format allows the reader to discern the total value of restricted contributions raised during the period as well as the total value of funds released from restriction. (Note that there are no expenses listed in the temporarily or permanently restricted columns; restrictions refer to contributed *income* only.) In monitoring the release from restriction, readers of financial statements are monitoring the organization's fulfillment of its promises to spend funds in proscribed ways or time frames. The essential accounting practice behind this concept is the tracking of expenses by <u>activity</u> so that the fulfillment of promises to spend can be tracked and reported on a monthly or quarterly basis. For instance, in order for DV to release funds that were restricted by the donor to the support groups program, DV must know how much it spent on the support groups program that month. In spending money the way they promised to in the original grant budget, DV is releasing funds from restriction.

A related accounting practice concerns the presentation of the organization's <u>net assets</u> by level of restriction. Net assets are what a nonprofit organization has left when it subtracts what it owes from what it owns or has title to. In the for-profit world, this is called "equity," but because nonprofits do not have shareholders or owners per se, they use the term net assets.

To help understand this concept, examine your personal net assets. On the asset side, you have things you own or have title to such as cash in the bank, a home, a car, and so forth. On the liability side are things you owe, such as mortgage payments, car payments, credit card payments, and so forth. To arrive at your personal net worth, you would add up the assets, add up the liabilities, and then subtract total liabilities from total assets.

What's different about nonprofits is that some of those assets may have donor restrictions on them. This in turn means that at any given time, some of the organization's net assets have restrictions on their use. Because net assets are where readers of financial statements look to determine the reserve of the organization—funds it could use to start a new program or buy a building, for instance—it is critical that they not blend unrestricted and restricted amounts in the presentation.

Figure 5. Statement of Activities

Domestic Violence Intervention & Prevention Agency
Statement of Activities
For the Nine Months Ending March 31, 2005

	❶ Unrestricted	❷ Temporarily Restricted	❸ Permanently Restricted	Total
Contributions	23,200	0	5,000	28,200
Fundraising events	118,304	0	0	118,304
Cost of fundraising events	(25,874)	0	0	(25,874)
Foundation grants	92,000	416,000	0	508,000
Total support	207,630	416,000	5,000 ❹	628,630
Government contracts	574,382	0	0	574,382
Interest and dividends	3,761	0	0	3,761
Unrealized gain (loss) on investments	(2,400)	0	0	(2,400)
Total revenue	575,743	0	0	575,743
Net assets released from restriction	322,335	❺(322,335)	0	0
Total income	1,105,708	93,665	5,000	1,204,373
Shelter Services	505,866	0 ❽	0	505,866
Support Groups	277,286	0	0	277,286
Administration	167,168	0	0	167,168
Fundraising	163,769	0	0	163,769
Total expenses	1,114,090	0	0	1,114,090
Change in net assets	❻(8,382)	93,665	5,000	90,283
Beginning net assets	283,690	326,004	100,000	709,694
Ending net assets	❼275,308	419,669	105,000	799,977

❶ Unrestricted funds—those funds without donor-imposed time or purpose restrictions.

❷ Temporarily restricted funds—those contributions with a time and/or programmatic restriction.

❸ Permanently restricted funds—those funds for which the principle must be held in perpetuity.

❹ Value of restricted contributions raised during the period.

❺ Value of funds released from restriction.

❻ Unrestricted change in net assets—income ($1,105,708) minus expense ($1,114,090) for the nine-month period.

❼ Unrestricted net assets—what a nonprofit organization has left when it subtracts what it owes from what it owns or has title to.

❽ Restricted refers to income, not expenses.

Figure 6, page 26, is DV's Statement of Financial Position—often called a balance sheet. This statement captures the cumulative net worth of DV since its inception. It tells the reader what DV owns, what it owes, and the difference, or net asset position, as of the date on the top of the statement. Notice that total net assets are equal to total assets minus total liabilities. But notice that the $799,977 in total net assets is broken down by restriction so that the reader can distinguish among funds that can be used in any way the organization desires and funds that represent promises to perform according to donor-

Figure 6. Statement of Financial Position

Domestic Violence Intervention & Prevention Agency
Statement of Financial Position
As of March 31, 2005

	Current YTD 3/31/05	Previous Year End 6/30/04
Assets		
Cash and equivalents	161,270	251,584
Investments	106,361	100,000
Contracts receivable	144,567	177,674
Grants receivable	315,000	124,000
Prepaid expenses	11,942	15,065
Total current assets	739,140	668,323
Buildings and improvements	180,000	180,000
Vehicles	32,750	32,750
Furniture and fixtures	48,955	48,955
Equipment	19,771	14,725
Total property and equipment	281,476	276,430
Less accumulated depreciation	(102,419)	(73,325)
Net property and equipment	179,057	203,105
Long-term deposits	3,589	3,589
Total non-current assets	3,589	3,589
Total assets	921,786 ❸	875,017
Liabilities and Net Assets		
Accounts payable	12,514	48,990
Accrued vacation	9,897	6,941
Current portion of long-term debt	14,259	13,457
Total current liabilities	36,670	69,388
Note payable (leasehold improvements)	99,398	109,392
Less current portion of long-term debt	(14,259)	(13,457)
Total liabilities	121,809	165,323
Unrestricted net assets	275,308 ⎤	283,690
Temporarily restricted net assets	419,669 ❷	326,004
Permanently restricted net assets	105,000 ⎦	100,000
Total net assets	❶ 799,977	709,694
Total liabilities and net assets	921,786 ❸	875,017

❶ Total net assets are equal to total assets ($921,786) minus total liabilities ($121,809). This is the cumulative net worth of DV since its inception, or net asset position as of the date on the top of the statement.

❷ DV's total net assets are broken down by restriction so that the reader can distinguish among funds that can be used in any way the organization desires and funds that represent promises to perform according to donor-approved budgets.

❸ Statement of Financial Position is often called a balance sheet because total liabilities ($121,809) plus total net assets ($799,977) must be equal to, or "balance," total assets ($921,786).

approved budgets. Without this information, your assessment of funds available to meet organizational goals will be incorrect. Because DV has unrestricted, temporarily restricted, and permanently restricted funds, its Statement of Financial Position shows the organization's net assets broken down by all three levels of restriction.

2. Functional classification of expenses

The second accounting practice to be aware of is called functional expenses classification. In the nonprofit world, there are three core functions that must be tracked: 1) program/mission-related activities; 2) administrative activities; and 3) fundraising activities. (Nonprofits incorporated with the IRS as membership organizations will have a fourth core function: membership development activities.) Auditors of nonprofit financial statements expect to see expense data by core function when they review your year-end statements, and the IRS requires that nonprofits report expenses functionally every year on the Form 990. In addition to these requirements, understanding the true costs of your core activities is good management, so you'll want to be sure that your accounting system is set up to track by function. Figure 7 provides definitions and examples of the three core function areas.

Figure 7. Functional Classifications of Expenses

Function	Definition	Examples
Program	Expenses related specifically to carrying out of your mission-related work	Salaries and benefits of program staff, program supplies, and the portion of occupancy costs incurred by program activities
Administration	Expenses not related to program or fundraising but that are essential to the organization's operation	Salaries and benefits of finance staff, a portion of the executive director's salary and benefits, board-related costs, and the portion of occupancy costs incurred by administrative staff
Fundraising	Expenses related to soliciting contributions for the organization	A portion of salary and benefits of any staff who participate in grantwriting, special events, cultivation and solicitation of individual or corporate donors, and the portion of occupancy costs incurred by fundraising staff

All nonprofits with paid staff have expenses in each of the core functions. For instance, it is important to recognize that even nonprofits that do not have development directors have fundraising expenses. Somebody is raising money; it may be the executive director and program directors, for instance. At DV, Elena charges 25 percent of her time and salary costs to the fundraising function because a quarter of her time is spent cultivating donors.

3. Employee time tracking

In most nonprofit organizations, staff have multiple job responsibilities. Typically, employee salaries and benefits are the largest category of expenses in a nonprofit organization. Therefore, having some mechanism in place for tracking how employees use their time across the functional categories described above—as well as across specific program activities—is essential to accurate financial reporting.

Time tracking systems vary widely across nonprofits depending on their size and mission type. We advise that small organizations with less defined job descriptions should still make an effort to get a handle on time tracking. For instance, employees may do a two-week time study each year (in which all staff track their time spent on various activities in half-hour intervals for a two-week period) to get a good sense for what kind of human resources (and therefore cost) are being dedicated to the organization's various activities. This data can then be used to establish how each employee's time will be charged to each activity for that year.

As organizations mature, they should institute a time sheet system that captures people's use of time across core activities year round. For instance, at DV, the time sheet's categories would be shelter, support groups, administration, fundraising, and common costs (those that will be allocated to the other activities each month). Each employee would turn in a time sheet for each pay period listing his or her hours in each category each day. Let's say that DV's program director reports 60 percent of her hours are spent on the shelter program and 40 percent on the support groups program. In this case, the bookkeeper would charge 60 percent of DV's program director's salary to the shelter program and 40 percent to the support group program. Without this information, the bookkeeper cannot confidently report how much the organization is spending on each of its activities.

Among nonprofits that receive temporarily restricted foundation grants and/or government contracts, time tracking often gets complicated by a "chicken or the egg" problem. When a position is budgeted in a grant or contract at 25 percent time, for instance, there is an incentive for organizations to "force" that to be true rather than relying on actual time data throughout the year. The only way to get better at budgeting people's time for grants and contracts purposes is to track the real thing and then use that data to inform the budgeting process. The bottom line is that funders want to pay for actual salary costs, not predetermined ones.

Having some mechanism in place for tracking how employees use their time is essential to accurate financial reporting.

4. Allocation of common costs

Notice that the final example in each of the core function areas in Figure 7 is "the portion of occupancy costs" incurred by the given functional area. Occupancy costs such as rent and custodial services are "common costs"—meaning that they are common to two or more activities in the organization. All staff and all activities use a portion of the physical space. Other common costs include telephone, office supplies, and copier lease payments. These are items that cannot be associated with just one activity but benefit them all. Allocation simply means to distribute these costs across activities. In order to properly report expenses functionally, an organization has to use allocation to get costs that are common to two or more activities spread appropriately.

As a consumer of financial statements, you need to understand whether and how these common costs get charged to each activity. The reason this is critical to good assessment is that if you are looking at a particular program's financial condition without considering its use of common costs, you will have a distortedly positive view. In fact, common costs can be as much as 50 percent or more of a program's full cost.

Figure 8, page 30, is DV's Statement of Functional Income and Expenses. This statement describes the income and expense year-to-date for each core activity of the organization. Notice that common costs are allocated below-the-line to all of the activities of the organization. That is, the common costs are distributed in one lump sum near the bottom of the report rather than by each line item. You can see that before the shelter program gets its allocation of common costs, its total expenditures are $372,501, but after allocation they are $505,866. That's more than an $130,000 difference. Your ability to confidently assess the financial condition of your activities depends on your understanding of the basic allocation practices that your bookkeeper is employing.

Allocation is accomplished using an allocation basis. The basis is the criteria for determining how much of the common costs each activity is charged. The most widely used allocation basis is the number of full-time equivalents (FTE)—or employees—in each activity. For instance, if your organization has ten full-time staff members and five of them work in Program A, Program A will be allocated 50 percent of your organization's common costs. Other possible allocation bases include percentage of total payroll costs per activity and percentage of activity costs before allocation. At DV, full-time equivalent (FTE) has been chosen as the allocation basis for common costs. As you can see, the allocation decisions are important and specific to individual organizations. You should feel comfortable talking with your bookkeeper about how allocation is or is not happening at your organization right now.

As a consumer of financial statements, you need to understand whether and how common costs get charged to each activity.

Figure 8. Statement of Functional Income and Expenses

Domestic Violence Intervention & Prevention Agency
Statement of Functional Income and Expenses
For the Nine Months Ending March 31, 2005

| | Program Activities | | Supporting Activities | | | |
	Shelter Services	Support Groups	Adminis-tration	Fund-raising	Common Costs	Total
Contributions	0	0	0	23,200	0	23,200
Fundraising events – net	0	0	0	92,430	0	92,430
Foundation grants	0	0	0	92,000	0	92,000
Total support	0	0	0	207,630	0	207,630
Government contracts	574,382	0	0	0	0	574,382
Interest and dividends	0	0	3,761	0	0	3,761
Unrealized gain (loss) on investments	0	0	(2,400)	0	0	(2,400)
Total revenue	574,382	0	1,361	0	0	575,743
Net assets released from restriction	0	312,315	0	10,020	0	322,335
Total income	574,382	312,315	1,361	217,650	0	1,105,708
Salaries	200,020	147,782	90,780	95,441	66,275	600,298
Payroll taxes	20,502	15,148	9,305	9,783	6,793	61,531
Employee benefits	0	0	954	0	61,959	62,913
Training	2,952	100	540	0	280	3,872
Personnel expenses	223,474	163,030	101,579	105,224	135,307	728,614
Accounting	0	0	14,160	0	0	14,160
Bank charges	0	0	2,745	0	0	2,745
Building expenses	0	0	0	0	20,800	20,800
Clients, direct assistance to	117,450	0	0	0	0	117,450
Conferences and meetings	741	8,463	1,706	1,247	2,047	14,204
Depreciation	0	0	0	0	25,260	25,260
Dues and subscriptions	582	1,886	39	125	0	2,632
Equipment rental/maintenance	0	0	0	0	2,515	2,515
Insurance	0	0	0	0	18,170	18,170
Interest	0	0	0	0	6,103	6,103
Other professional fees	15,600	7,280	2,500	0	4,600	29,980
Postage and delivery	0	0	0	2,886	6,488	9,374
Printing and copying	943	4,059	0	8,143	0	13,145
Supplies	11,648	8,686	0	1,888	15,336	37,558
Telephone	0	286	0	0	24,868	25,154
Travel	2,063	10,451	376	1,074	0	13,964
Utilities	0	0	0	0	32,262	32,262
Non-personnel expenses	149,027	41,111	21,526	15,363	158,449	385,476
Total specific costs	372,501	204,141	123,105	120,587	293,756	1,114,090
Common cost allocation (%)	45.40%	24.90%	15.00%	14.70%	-100.00%	0
Common cost allocation ($)	133,365	73,145	44,063	43,182	(293,756)	(0)
Total expenses after allocations	505,866	277,286	167,168	163,769	0	1,114,090
Change in net assets	68,516	35,029	(165,807)	53,881	0	(8,382)

❶ The Statement of Functional Income and Expenses describes the income and expenses year-to-date for each core activity of the organization. (For DV, this includes shelter services, support groups, administration, and fundraising.)

❷ Common costs—items that cannot be associated with just one activity, but benefit them all (such as rent, a copier lease, custodial services, or telephone service).

❸ Allocation basis—the criteria that determine how much common cost each activity is charged.

❹ Common costs are distributed below the line rather than by each line item.

❺ With allocation to the other activities, the common costs column is zeroed out.

5. Accrual basis accounting

The fifth accounting practice to be aware of is called <u>accrual</u>. Financial statements prepared on an accrual basis will include any income that your organization has earned or been promised (<u>accounts receivable</u>) but has not yet deposited in the bank as of the date on the top of the statements. Similarly, they will include all expenses that the organization has incurred but not yet paid (<u>accounts payable</u>) as of the date on the top of the statements. Except in the very smallest of organizations, accrual is the best practice because it gives a far more complete picture of the organization's financial condition. For instance, if you were reviewing statements that did not include thousands of dollars in unpaid bills (payables) due in two weeks, you would assume that you had more money to spend than you actually had—a very dangerous situation. Conversely, if you were unaware that a foundation had awarded you a $50,000 grant, you might make overly conservative spending decisions.

Accrual also ensures that <u>earned revenue</u>—such as tickets sales, service fees, and many government contracts—is matched with related expenses, regardless of whether the cash has been received. This is often referred to as the "<u>matching principle</u>," and it is necessary to assess the performance of a given activity in a given month or quarter. For instance, if DV provides shelter to 100 domestic violence survivors in January and their state contract pays them $100 for each month of shelter provided per client, then DV earned $10,000 in January despite the fact that the state check isn't received until February. If DV did not keep its books on an accrual basis, readers of the financial statements would assume that January was a disastrous month when in fact DV's work earned them $10,000 to cover shelter expenses. Notice that the DV Statement of Financial Position (Figure 6) has two types of receivables (<u>contracts receivable</u> and <u>grants receivable</u>) as well as accounts payable.

6. Capitalization and depreciation

Finally, the sixth accounting concept to be aware of is called <u>capitalization and depreciation</u>. This accounting practice allows organizations to spread the cost of capital acquisitions such as telephone systems and computer networks across their estimated useful life. For instance, if DV buys new furniture for its shelter site for $15,000, it will add $15,000 to the furniture and equipment asset line of its Statement of Financial Position to note that it now owns an asset with a value of $15,000. Let's assume that DV ascribes a useful life of five years to the furniture. For each of the next five years, DV will depreciate the value of the furniture by $3,000 until its full depreciation is captured on their Statement of Financial Position. In other words, at the end of five years, the full $15,000 value of the furniture will be offset in the depreciation line on the statement; in accounting terms, the furniture no longer has material financial value.

Except in the very smallest of organizations, accrual is the best practice because it gives a far more complete picture of the organization's financial condition.

Figure 9. Depreciation Schedule

Domestic Violence Intervention & Prevention Agency
Depreciation Schedule
As of March 31, 2005

Item Description	Date Acquired	Cost	Expected Years	Book Value 6/30/04	2004–05		
					Dep. Expense	Accum. Dep.	Book Value 3/31/05
Van #1	Jul-01	32,750	5	13,100	4,913	24,563	8,187
Computer #1	Oct-01	2,412	3	201	201	2,412	0
Computer #2	Oct-01	1,422	3	119	119	1,422	0
Copier (capital lease)	Feb-02	3,000	5	1,550	450	1,900	1,100
Leasehold improvements	May-02	180,000	15	154,000	9,000	35,000	145,000
Furniture and fixtures	Jun-02	48,955	5	28,557	7,343	27,741	21,214
Laser printer	Aug-02	2,096	3	756	524	1,864	232
File server	Nov-02	7,286	3	3,238	1,822	5,870	1,416
Computer #3	Jun-03	1,286	3	821	322	787	499
Computer #4	Sep-03	1,057	3	764	264	557	500
Computer #5	Dec-04	1,212	3	0	303	303	909
Total		❶ 281,476		203,106	25,261	❷ 102,419	❸ 179,057

❶ Purchase price or property and equipment as listed on the Statement of Financial Position (Figure 6).

❷ Accumulated depreciation total.

❸ The current book value of the property and equipment.

The key thing to understand is that at the time of purchase, DV did write a check for $15,000, thus lowering their cash total, but in capitalizing the shelter furniture, they converted one kind of asset (cash) into another kind (furniture and equipment). Therefore, the depreciation of $3,000 for each of five years is a non-cash expense. Fixed assets like furniture and equipment are listed on the Statement of Financial Position with the corresponding depreciation total immediately below. This presentation allows you to recognize when such assets are nearing complete depreciation; this may indicate that you will have to invest in new equipment in the near term.

Look at the asset section of DV's Statement of Financial Position (Figure 6) to find their property and equipment. Its total purchase price was $281,476, but depreciation of (102,419) makes its current value $179,057. Figure 9 is DV's depreciation schedule. All organizations should keep such a schedule to track the acquisition and subsequent depreciation of their capitalized assets.

While there are many more concepts in accounting, these six are fundamental in a majority of community-based nonprofit businesses. They are concepts that managers, executives, and board members need to have a working understanding of in order to trust and make use of the financial reports they receive. If the practices are not in place at your organization, we suggest that you sit down with your bookkeeper and find out why. There are two goals for this discussion: first, to identify whether one or more of the practices is not relevant to your organization, and second, to identify any training needs your finance staff may have. For instance, if your organization receives no temporarily or permanently restricted contributions, then that would explain why you're not seeing that language on your financial statements. On the other hand, you may receive such contributions but not see them presented properly because your bookkeeper has not been trained in this aspect of nonprofit finance.

Accounting Systems

Though many hear the term "accounting system" and think immediately of software, in fact the heart of an accounting system is what's called the chart of accounts. The chart of accounts is the set of numerical labels that your organization uses to describe its assets, liabilities, net assets, income, and expenses. In a chart of accounts, you also give a numerical label to your core program, administration, and fundraising activities. Many organizations also give a numerical label to their key funding sources such as grants and contracts. Non-finance staff, including the executive director, interact with the chart of accounts in two ways. First, they use the numerical labels to code the expenses they authorize. Second, all of the reports that an accounting system can produce are based on the chart of accounts. If a consumer of financial information wants a particular activity to be presented in a financial report, it requires that the activity be assigned a number in the chart of accounts. At DV, the chart of accounts has three types of labels or segments: account, activity, and funding source. For instance, DV's bookkeeper would enter a bill for shelter supplies by entering the numerical labels for the supplies account, the shelter activity, and the shelter's government contract. It is critical that the financial leaders of a nonprofit business understand the chart of accounts and influence it to ensure meaningful financial reporting.

Still, bookkeepers often feel limited by the accounting software they are using and may point to it as the reason they cannot produce meaningful financial statements. Fortunately there are now resources to help people use inexpensive business products like Intuit's QuickBooks Pro in a nonprofit context. There are also nonprofit-specific packages that are relatively inexpensive and more than adequate for most community-based nonprofits. As organizations grow, they can consider the more expensive and robust modular accounting

Though many hear the term "accounting system" and think immediately of software, in fact the heart of an accounting system is what's called the chart of accounts.

New accounting software may make report production more efficient, but it will never make up for the fact that someone does not have the proper training in nonprofit accounting.

software products designed to be responsive to such nonprofit issues as grant tracking and functional expense allocation (see Appendix C, Resources, for more information about accounting software options). The important thing about software is this: If your bookkeeper or finance manager understands the accounting concepts presented in this chapter, he or she can create reports in basic spreadsheet software such as Microsoft Excel using data from any accounting software. In other words, new accounting software may make report production more efficient, but it will never make up for the fact that someone does not have the proper training in nonprofit accounting.

Choosing accounting software—for the first time or as an upgrade from the system you have now—is a seemingly technical event that executives should nonetheless play a role in. As the financial leader of your organization, you should be concerned with the following issues when purchasing an accounting system:

1. Do we actually need new software or are we inadequately trained to maximize our current system?

2. Are we buying a product that is consistent with our needs and staff capacity, or are we over- or underbuying?

3. Are we using the purchase process as a platform for updating and streamlining our financial tracking procedures (chart of accounts)?

4. Is the staff person coordinating the purchase adequately involving key consumers of the system's reports: program managers, development mangers, board treasurer, and executive director?

If your organization is large enough to have paid finance staff, you should make the senior finance staff person the project manager on an accounting software purchase. She or he can convene key consumers to learn what reporting needs are currently unmet; restructure the chart of accounts accordingly; investigate appropriate products in your price range; and work on setup and implementation. As the financial leader, you should be interviewed as a consumer and make the final decision to buy or not based on the project manager's recommendations. Though you will not actually use the accounting system in a hands-on way, on behalf of yourself and the other key consumers on staff and board, you need to exercise leadership around the quality of your organization's accounting system.

Evaluate Your Staffing, Practices, and Systems

Take the organizational evaluation in Figure 10 on page 36 to consider the current quality of finance staffing, practices, and systems at your nonprofit. Elena's answers and comments are highlighted for your reference under "comments." A complete blank version of the evaluation tool can be found in Appendix B.

Nonprofit Lifecycles and Financial Practices

Do you lead a young organization that has no finance staff, but is relying on its volunteer board treasurer to keep the books? Or perhaps this chapter is the first time you are hearing accounting terms like "accrual" and "restricted contributions." We want to stress that organizations have natural lifecycles—from the start-up phase through maturity and renewal.[2] The sophistication of financial practices evolves as an organization grows—usually because key staff and board eventually become dissatisfied with the very limited financial information they are getting and decide that they need more in order to make good decisions. The reporting demands of foundation and government funders can also spur the development of stronger systems.

In our workshops and consulting practice, we encounter many nonprofit organizations that do wonderful things in the community but have yet to staff their finance function adequately or develop a strong accounting system. If you are in this boat, don't dismay. It is natural for start-up organizations to be almost myopically focused on mission and survival. Developing systems comes a bit later, unless it happens to be the strength or passion of the founding leaders.

What's presented in this chapter and throughout this book are what we believe to be best practices, but you may not be able to implement them all at once or even in one year. Pay particular attention to how Elena, the executive director of our case study organization DV, responds to the Red/Yellow/Green Evaluation Tools at the end of each chapter. Her comments will give you insight into how that organization's practices have evolved.

[2] For more on organization lifecycles, see *The Five Life Stages of Nonprofit Organizations*, by Judith Sharken Simon, published in 2001 by Fieldstone Alliance.

Summary

While you as a nonprofit executive may not typically be involved in a hands-on way with your organization's finance systems, you must ensure that those systems are in place. Proper staffing, appropriate accounting practices, and a strong accounting system are the foundation upon which you can develop financial leadership. Together they ensure that the right processes are in place to generate accurate and meaningful financial data for the organization's decision makers. If an organization has mostly "red" findings in its organizational evaluation, staff and board will struggle to execute the leadership practices outlined in the rest of this book. In that case, leadership should prioritize getting its fundamental financial infrastructure in place.

Chapter 2 helped you understand why accurate data and good systems are important. Chapter 3 will help you use that information to assess the overall financial health of your organization.

Figure 10. Accurate Financial Data Assessment

Category	Red	Yellow	Green	Comments	Action Plan
Accounting Software	The accounting software is inadequate for the organization's tracking and reporting needs.	The accounting software is adequate for the organization's tracking and reporting needs, but not well implemented.	The accounting software is adequate for the organization's tracking and reporting needs and has been implemented to support optimal financial reporting.	DV has outgrown its accounting system.	Convert to a system that better meets our needs in the next 12–18 months.
Staffing	The providers of financial reports to management and board are not trained in the specifics of nonprofit accounting.	The providers of financial reports to management and board are in the process of being trained in the specifics of nonprofit accounting.	The providers of financial reports to management and board are well trained in the specifics of nonprofit accounting.	Our finance staff has experience in the for-profit sector; we are all learning about nonprofit accounting together.	Continued staff development.
Accounting Practices	None of the five key accounting practices are being followed.	Most of the five key accounting practices are being followed.	Each of the five key accounting practices is being followed.	Given the constraints of our accounting system, we have some trouble reporting contributions by restriction.	Until system conversion, continue to use spreadsheet program for monthly reporting.
Internal Controls	Internal controls are not in place.	Some controls are in place but leadership has not prioritized optimal internal controls.	Because of leadership's emphasis on accountability and transparency, internal controls are prioritized and ensured	We have recently created a fiscal policies and procedures manual that outlines our internal control procedures.	Update manual as needed.
Chart of Accounts	The chart of accounts is managed solely by the bookkeeper and does not reflect the current activities of the organization.	The chart of accounts is fairly reflective of current activities, but needs updating.	The chart of accounts is reviewed and understood by key staff and board. It reflects current activities.	As part of our annual budgeting process, we review the chart of accounts.	Update chart as needed.
Financial Reporting	The content of the monthly financial package varies and may consist of a simple overall income and expense report.	The monthly financial package includes (at least) a Statement of Activities and a Statement of Position.	The monthly financial package includes a Statement of Position, a Budgeted Statement of Activities, a Statement of Functional Income and Expense, and an updated Cash Flow Forecast.	We are quite satisfied with the monthly reporting package, but our reports are produced outside the accounting system.	Ensure that new accounting software package can produce monthly reports in the format required.

3. Assessing Your Organization's Financial Health

I f, based on the organizational evaluation completed in Chapter 2, you have determined that you can trust the financial data you have about your nonprofit business, then you can move on to assessment. Among nonprofit leaders who don't bring a finance background to their work, assessment is typically the weakest part of their financial leadership skill set. This is because it requires the ability to read and understand financial statements—something that for many non-finance people is a scary proposition. But assessment is critical to doing good planning and communicating, so though you may be tempted, do not skip ahead. We have designed this chapter around the questions that you'll need to be able to answer as your organization's financial leader, and we are going to show you where to find the answers.

The Financial Leader's Key Assessment Questions

As a leader, you have three overarching questions to ask about the financial health of your organization:

1. What are our immediate financial strengths and vulnerabilities?

   This area of inquiry includes your ability to pay your bills and salaries, how the organization is performing compared with its annual budget, and the performance of your investments. These are the most basic and fundamental questions a financial leader must be able to answer. When an organization is in or approaching financial crisis, it is these issues that keep an executive director up at night.

2. **What are our long-term financial strengths and vulnerabilities?**

   This is the longer-range view and the most strategic of the three key questions. Financial leaders must anticipate a host of factors that can impact organizational financial health now and in the coming years. The concerns here include: Do we have an adequate financial reserve? Are our core programs performing well financially? Do we have a sustainable portfolio of activities? Are we positioned well given the likely trends in funding our work?

3. **Do our constituents perceive us as efficient and competitive?**

   This area of inquiry includes the cost of your key programmatic outputs/ outcomes, your percentage of funds spent on overhead costs, and your cost to raise a dollar. With the increasing emphasis among donors and the media on how nonprofit dollars are being spent, it is critical that organizations track their own measures of efficiency and make adjustments as necessary.

Using DV's story and financial statements, let's now take a closer look at each of these questions and how you can go about answering them.

1. What are our immediate financial strengths and vulnerabilities?

While there are a number of assessment questions that may be applicable at some organizations, these four are widely relevant and get at the fundamental issues facing most community-based organizations:

- Do we have sufficient resources to pay our bills and staff salaries?
- Is the timing of our receipt and disbursement of cash (cash flow) a challenge?
- Are we on track with our financial plan (budget) for this year?
- Are we investing wisely?

Do we have sufficient resources to pay our bills and staff salaries?

Much of an organization's financial strength (or vulnerability) is reflected on its Statement of Financial Position, or balance sheet. Unfortunately, many nonprofit leaders are not comfortable reading this report. Their discomfort leaves them unable to answer some fundamental assessment questions. For instance, to determine if you'll be able to pay your bills and make payroll, you need to look at your Statement of Financial Position. Just by doing a quick comparison of current assets and current liabilities, you will get a sense for this one. Remember, assets are things you own (like cash) and liabilities are things you owe (like bills and salaries). When we say "current" in reference to assets and liabilities, we mean available (assets) or due (liabilities) within the year. Naturally, you want to have more assets than liabilities. Let's look at Figure 11, DV's Statement of Financial Position, to explore assets and liabilities.

Figure 11. Statement of Financial Position

Domestic Violence Intervention & Prevention Agency
Statement of Financial Position
As of March 31, 2005

	Current YTD 3/31/05	Previous Year End 6/30/04
Assets		
Cash and equivalents	161,270	251,584
Investments	106,361	100,000
Contracts receivable	144,567	177,674
Grants receivable	315,000	124,000
Prepaid expenses	11,942	15,065
Total current assets ❶	739,140	668,323
Buildings and improvements	180,000	180,000
Vehicles	32,750	32,750
Furniture and fixtures	48,955	48,955
Equipment	19,771	14,725
Total property and equipment	281,476	276,430
Less accumulated depreciation	(102,419)	(73,325)
Net property and equipment	179,057	203,105
Long-term deposits	3,589	3,589
Total non-current assets	3,589	3,589
Total assets	921,786	875,017
Liabilities and Net Assets		
Accounts payable	12,514	48,990
Accrued vacation	9,897	6,941
Current portion of long-term debt	14,259	13,457
Total current liabilities ❷	36,670	69,388
Mortgage payable	99,398	109,392
Less current portion of long-term debt	(14,259)	(13,457)
Total liabilities	121,809	165,323
Unrestricted net assets	275,308	283,690
Temporarily restricted net assets	419,669	326,004
Permanently restricted net assets	105,000	100,000
Total net assets	799,977	709,694
Total liabilities and net assets	921,786	875,017

❶ Current assets—things (like cash) you own that are available within one year.

❷ Current liabilities—things (like bills and salaries) that are due within the year.

❸ Given DV's receivable balance of $326,942, cash flow (the timing of the receipt and use of cash) may be an issue.

Let's assess DV's ability to pay its bills. We create a ratio, or comparison of two numbers, using the current assets and the current liabilities. This ratio is called a current ratio.

Current Ratio:

Total Current Assets
―――――――――――――
Total Current Liabilities

$$\frac{\text{Total DV Current Assets} = \$739,140}{\text{Total DV Current Liabilities} = \$36,670} = \frac{20}{1}$$

In other words, for every $1 that DV owes in the short term, it has $20 in cash and receivables. Note that the vast majority of DV's current assets are in fact grants and contracts receivable as opposed to cash. If we wanted to calculate this ratio with *only* cash and investments in hand, it would look like this:

Quick Ratio (cash only):

Total Cash and Investments
―――――――――――――――
Total Current Liabilities

$$\frac{\text{Total DV Cash and Investments} = \$267,631}{\text{Total DV Current Liabilities} = \$36,670} = \frac{7.3}{1}$$

In this case, you would say for every $1 that DV owes in the short term, it has $7.30 in the bank. So, the ratio is still a comfortable 7.3:1. The closer an organization gets to a 1:1 ratio, the more precarious it is. Indeed we have worked with some nonprofit organizations that are in financial crisis and have fewer assets than liabilities (for example, a ratio of 0.5:1.) For DV though, we can say that liquidity, or having cash available to cover liabilities, is a financial strength.

Is the timing of our receipt and disbursement of cash (cash flow) a challenge?

A related assessment issue is cash flow. Cash flow refers to the timing of the receipt and use of cash in an organization. Even if a nonprofit is working with a balanced or surplus budget for the year, because of the timing of its income, it may experience challenges during certain parts of the year in making payroll and paying vendors. There are many instances in nonprofit businesses of delayed receipt of income. For example, some government contracts reimburse nonprofits for their expenses two or more months after those expenses are incurred; individual donors may pledge funds and make payments over the course of a year or more; once awarded, foundation grants may come in installments several months after the grant period has begun. In these cases, it isn't enough for a board to approve a budget; the staff also needs to do a cash flow analysis to determine if and when the organization may have to use a line of credit to tide itself over until cash is received. If this assessment predicts there will be difficult months during the year and a line of credit is not available to the nonprofit, expenses may have to be delayed to match up with the receipt of funds.

In the case of DV, the cash flow analysis predicted that several months of the fiscal year would be difficult due to a slow-paying government contract. At this point in the year, the Statement of Financial Position (Figure 11) shows that DV has a contracts receivable balance of $144,567. DV does not have a line of credit that it can draw on during these slow periods in order to make payroll and pay vendors. Given the organization's reliance on government contracts, DV may consider applying for a line of credit in the following fiscal year and/or negotiating with the funding agency the option to draw an advance on their contract.

Are we on track with our financial plan (budget) for this year?

In a given year, another measure of strength or weakness is the comparison of actual financial results to planned financial results. Each month the financial leader reviews a financial statement that includes separate columns for the actual performance in the past month, actual performance year-to-date, and the budget for the year. The financial leader is looking for variances—or meaningful differences between the actual figures and the planned figures. Assessing progress on financial plans each month gives the organization ample time to respond to unanticipated financial performance issues. Staff can decide to be more aggressive in foundation grantwriting, or to cut back on a certain group of expenses, for example. On the other hand, when a budget is approved but never used in the monthly tracking of financial progress, leaders are at risk for missing clear evidence of impending financial problems until it is too late.

Note that the DV Budgeted Statement of Activity (Figure 12, page 42) includes this kind of budget information. The variance column alerts the reader to the fact that the organization is spending very close to its plan, but has not brought in as much money at this point in the year as it had projected. Three-quarters of the way through the year, the actual year-to-date contributions income is $23,200, but the total budgeted contributions for the year are $58,000. While the organization is 75 percent of the way through the year, it has raised just 40 percent of its budgeted goal for this type of income. Put another way, the relationship between income and expenses that the organization set out to achieve—a small surplus—is not happening. To end the year with that planned surplus, income will have to pick up for the rest of the year or expenses will have to be cut down to align with the new income expectations.

Running a significant and unplanned deficit is one piece of data that could indicate vulnerability, or in the worst-case scenario, an impending crisis. In DV's case, does the fact that they are running a small unplanned deficit mean that DV is approaching financial crisis? Organizations that have larger reserves can "afford" to incur an operating deficit in a given year because they have accumulated unrestricted money to tap. In your personal life, this would be akin to using part of your savings built up in prior years to compensate for the fact that you are spending more than you are earning this year. On the other hand, when

Assessing progress on financial plans each month gives the organization ample time to respond to unanticipated financial performance issues.

Figure 12. Budgeted Statement of Activity – Unrestricted

Domestic Violence Intervention & Prevention Agency
Budgeted Statement of Activity – Unrestricted
For the Nine Months Ending March 31, 2005

	YTD Actual	YTD Budget	➊ Variance B/(W)	Annual Budget	➍ $ Remaining	% Remaining
Contributions	23,200	43,500	(20,300)	58,000	34,800	60%
Fundraising events - net	92,430	93,750	(1,320)	125,000	32,570	26%
Foundation grants	92,000	86,250	5,750	115,000	23,000	20%
Total support	207,630	223,500	(15,870)	298,000	90,370	30%
Government contracts	574,382	577,850	(3,468)	770,467	196,085	25%
Interest and dividends	3,761	4,313	(552)	5,750	1,989	35%
Unrealized gain (loss) on investments	(2,400)	–	(2,400)	–	2,400	n/a
Total revenue	575,743	582,163	(6,420)	776,217	200,474	26%
Net assets released from restriction ➌	322,335	339,750	(17,415)	453,000	130,665	29%
Total income	1,105,708	1,145,413	(39,705)	1,527,217	421,509	28%
Shelter Services	505,866	502,478	(3,388)	669,971	164,105	24%
Support Groups	277,286	288,695	11,408	384,926	107,640	28%
Administration	167,168	156,025	(11,144)	208,033	40,865	20%
Fundraising	163,769	161,834	(1,935)	215,779	52,010	24%
Total expenses	1,114,090	1,109,032	(5,058)	1,478,709	364,619	25%
Change in net assets	➋ (8,382)	36,381	(44,763)	48,508	56,890	117%
Beginning net assets	283,690	283,690	–	283,690		
Ending net assets	275,308	320,071	(44,763)	332,198	56,890	17%

B = Better than budgeted
(W) = Worse than budgeted

➊ The variance column alerts readers to differences between planned (budgeted) and actual income and expenses for the period.

➋ An unplanned deficit can indicate vulnerability if the organization has no "reserve" of unrestricted money.

➌ Net assets released from restriction—money spent in a manner that satisfies donor purpose and/or time restrictions.

➍ These columns show the reader the total dollars and percentage of dollars left to raise or spend in the remaining three months of the fiscal year.

an organization has little cumulative net worth, even a relatively small deficit can mean a financial crisis. At DV, the current operating deficit is potentially important to watch and respond to because the organization does not have ample savings built up in prior years with which to compensate for the deficit. In other words, its margin for error is quite small.

Are we investing wisely?

Finally, as a financial leader, you want to work with your board to ensure that your organization is investing wisely. Over time, unrestricted earned interest can be an important part of your reserves. The goal is to get the best possible return on idle cash—the amount of which is anticipated through careful cash flow analysis. Rather than letting it sit in a checking account or minimal interest savings account, cash not needed for operations in the short term may be invested in certificates of deposits (CDs), treasury bonds, or other investment strategies. Like all investors, nonprofits have to balance the desire for a high return with their need to keep funds liquid and available for emergencies.

If a nonprofit has an endowment—a principle of permanently restricted funds meant to generate interest for the nonprofit indefinitely—how that investment is managed is critical. In this case, the organization may employ an outside portfolio manager or advisor. Additionally, some nonprofit boards develop polices that restrict certain investments in the stock market (seen as too risky) or in certain elements of the stock market that contradict organizational values. Within the parameters established by the board of directors, a financial leader should strive to maximize return on investments.

If a nonprofit has an endowment—a principle of permanently restricted funds meant to generate interest for the nonprofit indefinitely—how that investment is managed is critical.

In DV's case, look to the Net Assets section of the Statement of Financial Position (Figure 11) to see that DV has $106,361 invested. Next, look to the Statement of Activities (Figure 5) to see what kind of return DV is getting on this investment. The income line items "interest and dividends" and "unrealized gains/losses on investment" tell us that DV made $1,361 on its investments for this period. An appropriate question from the executive director and board treasurer is always, "Could we have done better?"

2. What are our long-term financial strengths and vulnerabilities?

Even as a financial leader considers the present, she works to anticipate the future so that she can position the organization for the best financial and programmatic health. This is as much art as science and requires a range of skills and tactics that goes far beyond financial assessment, including maintaining strong relationships with funders and staying ahead of the curve on the issues your nonprofit exists to address. Let's look at a few strategic assessment questions that a financial leader should consider because they have implications for the organization's health in coming years:

- Do we have a comfortable liquid operating reserve?
- How are our core activities performing financially?
- Are we recovering costs from our key funders?
- Do we have a sustainable portfolio of activities?
- Are our income streams stable and sufficiently diverse?

Do we have a comfortable liquid operating reserve?

A liquid operating reserve is unrestricted money that the organization has accumulated over time beyond what it needs to pay its immediate bills and other commitments. Having a liquid reserve is valuable for many reasons. Reserve funds can be used to make up for the unanticipated loss of a key funding source or the under-performance of a special event in a given budget year; they can be used to buy things not covered in existing grants or contracts such as equipment and buildings; they can be invested to generate additional money for the organization. It is important to recognize that the only way for an organization to build a liquid operating reserve is to generate more unrestricted money than it spends. Remember, temporarily restricted funds cannot be accumulated in a reserve, but instead have to be spent according to donor stipulations.

The size of your liquid operating reserve is a measure of strength or vulnerability because it represents your rainy-day fund—your ability to weather financial challenges and invest in new opportunities. Nonprofits that have a "culture of scarcity" may be unwilling to reserve even modest funds rather than direct them to immediate programmatic needs. Indeed, such organizations may not think to *budget* for a reserve—that is, intentionally raise more unrestricted money than the organization needs for the year's operating plan. But in nonprofits with strong financial leadership, building and maintaining a reserve is an essential financial goal.

At the same time, nonprofits do not exist to accumulate money. Beyond a certain level of comfort, accumulating money that could be spent on your mission work is not responsible. In fact, the Better Business Bureau's Wise Giving Alliance (www.give.org) recommends that nonprofits have no more than three times their current operating budget accumulated in liquid unrestricted net assets, or reserve. So for example, if your organization is going to spend $250,000 this year, the Wise Giving Alliance suggests that you not have more than $750,000 in liquid unrestricted net assets.

In nonprofits with strong financial leadership, building and maintaining a reserve is an essential financial goal.

Now, let's look at DV's liquid operating reserve. It is easiest to talk about reserve in terms of months of expenses. This puts the reserve in context. So, we compare how much liquid unrestricted net assets DV has with a typical month's budgeted expenses. This will tell us how long DV could operate using *only* the unrestricted net assets it has on hand. Look to DV's Statement of Financial Position (Figure 11) to find total unrestricted net assets ($275,308). Next, subtract from this total the net property and equipment ($179,057) so that you do not include non-cash items in your calculation of liquid reserves. Now look to DV's Budgeted Statement of Activities (Figure 12) to find a typical month's expenses. Since Figure 12 captures nine months of expense, we can divide total expenses ($1,114,090) by nine to find a good approximation of DV's typical monthly expense.

$$\frac{\text{Unrestricted net assets - Total fixed assets} = \$96,251}{\text{Typical monthly expenses} = \$123,788} = \frac{.78}{1}$$

> **Reserve Ratio:**
>
> Unrestricted Net Assets
> – Total Fixed Assets
> _____
> Typical Monthly Expenses

In using only the unrestricted net assets, we exclude those net assets DV has committed to spend (temporarily restricted funds) or retain indefinitely (permanently restricted funds). The ratio tells us that DV has less than one month of reserve. Generally, nonprofits should strive to have 3–6 months of reserve, so for DV, reserve is a weakness. You will recall that in the discussion of budget variance, we noted that a significant unplanned deficit for the current year would be a problem for DV because of this relatively low reserve.

Growing a reserve to 3–6 months of operating expenses is a challenge that many small organizations may never meet. Getting to one month of reserves may be a good stretch goal for some organizations. The key point is to know what it takes to build a reserve (unrestricted money) and to recognize how critical good financial planning and discipline are when you have a small margin for error.

How are core activities performing financially?

As we have discussed, nonprofits have different kinds of core activities: mission-related, administrative, and fundraising. Unlike for-profit businesses, nonprofit businesses frequently elect to maintain activities that lose money. At the same time, if a nonprofit business has only these money-losing activities it cannot survive. Like any business, it needs to generate surpluses somewhere in order to maintain even a small reserve as well as to invest in such things as facilities and new, unfunded program ideas. The name of the game for a nonprofit leader is to arrive at the right mix—or portfolio—of activities that best accomplishes mission and maintains the financial viability of the organization.

Figure 13. Statement of Functional Income and Expenses – Summarized

Domestic Violence Intervention & Prevention Agency
Statement of Functional Income and Expenses – Summarized
For the Nine Months Ending March 31, 2005

	Program Activities		Supporting Activities			
	Shelter Services	Support Groups	Admin- istration	Fund- raising	Common Costs	Total
Contributions	0	0	0	23,200	0	23,200
Fundraising events - net	0	0	0	92,430	0	92,430
Foundation grants	0	0	0	92,000	0	92,000
Total support	0	0	0	207,630	0	207,630
Government contracts	574,382	0	0	0	0	574,382
Interest and dividends	0	0	3,761	0	0	3,761
Unrealized gain (loss) on investments	0	0	(2,400)	0	0	(2,400)
Total revenue	574,382	0	1,361	0	0	575,743
Net assets released from restriction	0	312,315	0	10,020	0	322,335
Total income	574,382	312,315	1,361	217,650	0	1,105,708
Personnel expenses	223,474	163,030	101,579	105,224	135,307	728,614
Non-personnel expenses	149,027	41,111	21,526	15,363	158,449	385,476
Total specific costs	372,501	204,141	123,105	120,587	293,756	1,114,090
Common cost allocation	133,365	73,145	44,063	43,182	(293,756)	(0)
Total expenses before admin allocation	505,866	277,286	167,168	163,769	0	1,114,090
Administrative cost allocation (%)	53.40%	29.30%	-100.00%	17.30%	0	(0)
Administrative cost allocation ($)	89,268	48,980	(167,168)	28,920	0	(0)
Total expenses after allocations	595,134	326,266	0	192,689	0	1,114,090
Change in net assets	(20,752)	(13,951)	1,361	❷ 24,961	0	(8,382)

The financial data shown is marked with ❶ above the column headers.

❶ Financial data is broken down by DV's activities, allowing readers to see which activities are moneymakers and which are money-losers.

❷ The fundraising activity of a nonprofit should be a money-maker—an activity that brings in more money than it spends.

In order for financial leaders to assess the financial performance of core activities, they must be able to see financial reports where financial data is broken down by core activity. This is why DV's Statement of Functional Income and Expenses is so critical—and why as the financial leader of your organization you'll want a report of similar format. Like many nonprofit businesses, DV has some moneymaking activities and some money-losers.

Typically, the <u>administrative activity</u> of a nonprofit will be a money-loser; that is, in and of itself it does not generate sufficient funds to cover its costs. Indeed the only income that is booked to the administrative activity, if any, is interest earned on various accounts and investments. So the administrative column of the Statement of Functional Income and Expense will always show a deficit. On the other hand, the fundraising activity should be a money-maker—an activity that by bringing in more than it spends can subsidize other activities (like administration or certain programs). Program activities will vary in their financial performance. Some programs are notoriously difficult to fund, while others may have ample appeal and therefore support from donors.

Look across the bottom row of DV's Statement of Functional Income and Expense (Figure 13) to determine which of its activities is generating a surplus and which a deficit. As it should ideally, the fundraising activity is showing a surplus. DV's core programs—shelter and support groups—are generating modest deficits. As discussed in Chapter 1's review of foundational financial leadership principles, the financial leader of a nonprofit has to be able to look at this mix of activities and adjust it as necessary to ensure the financial health of the organization overall. For instance, what if next year the government contract for the shelter activity gets reduced, leading to a larger deficit for the shelter activity? The financial leader may assess that DV cannot absorb additional deficits and determine that costs—and shelter nights provided—must be reduced. Or in the case of the support group activity, DV might explore adding a fee-for-service component, for instance asking people who can afford it to pay $20 per session. If this resulted in the support group activity covering its costs, this would contribute to the financial health of the organization overall. These kinds of adjustments can happen because of ongoing assessment of financial performance at the level of activity.

Notice that in the Activity by Funding Sources report (Figure 14, pages 48–49), common costs are not shown in a separate cost pool and allocated below-the-line the way they are on DV's internal Statement of Activities (see Figure 5). This is because in preparing budgets for funders, common costs are generally not presented any differently than the other costs of executing a program or activity. So although internally DV uses a common costs pool for allocation, they still need to be able to track which funders are covering common costs. In this view, common costs are contained in the appropriate line items.

Figure 14. Activity by Funding Sources

Domestic Violence Intervention & Prevention Agency
Support Groups by Funding Sources
For the Nine Months Ending March 31, 2005

	Budget 100%	Support Groups - YTD Actual			Allen Foundation ❶	
		Specific	Common	Total	Budget 28%	Actual YTD
Contributions	–			–	–	–
Fundraising events - net	–			–	–	–
Foundation grants	–			–	–	–
Total support	–			–	–	–
Government contracts	–			–	–	–
Interest and dividends	–			–	–	–
Unrealized gain (loss) on investments	–			–	–	–
Total revenue	–			–	–	–
Net assets released from restriction	443,000			312,315	123,000	109,437
Total income	443,000			312,315	123,000	109,437
Salaries	221,138	147,782	16,502	164,284	75,000	63,150
Payroll taxes	22,667	15,148	1,691	16,839	6,000	6,874
Employee benefits	24,140	–	15,428	15,428	7,000	7,435
Training	800	100	70	170	300	74
Personnel expenses	268,745	163,030	33,691	196,721	88,300	77,533
Accounting	–	–	–	–	–	–
Bank charges	–	–	–	–	–	–
Building expenses	7,500	–	5,179	5,179	1,500	1,500
Clients, direct assistance to	–	–	–	–	–	–
Conferences and meetings	10,600	8,463	510	8,973	10,000	9,000
Depreciation	16,200	–	6,290	6,290	500	500
Dues and subscriptions	2,300	1,886	–	1,886	500	500
Equipment rental/maintenance	960	–	626	626	–	–
Insurance	6,900	–	4,524	4,524	157	157
Interest	2,402	–	❸ 1,520	1,520	–	–
Other professional fees	9,500	7,280	1,145	8,425	–	–
Postage and delivery	2,400	–	1,616	1,616	1,000	973
Printing and copying	5,000	4,059	–	4,059	–	–
Supplies	16,480	8,686	3,819	12,505	–	–
Telephone	9,540	286	6,192	6,478	2,500	2,500
Travel	15,000	10,451	–	10,451	–	–
Utilities	11,400	–	8,033	8,033	2,500	2,500
Non-personnel expenses	116,182	41,111	39,454	80,565	18,657	17,630
Total expenses before admin	384,927	204,141	73,145	277,286	106,957	95,163
Admin expenses ❹	63,020			48,980	16,043	14,274
Total expenses after allocations	447,947			326,266	123,000	109,437
Change in net assets	(4,947)			(13,951)	0	–

Belle Foundation		All Funders		Over/
Budget 71%	Actual YTD	Budget 99%	Actual YTD	(Under) -1%
–	–	–	–	0
–	–	–	–	0
–	–	–	–	0
–	–	–	–	–
–	–	–	–	0
–	–	–	–	0
–	–	–	–	0
–	–	–	–	–
320,000	202,878	443,000	312,315	0
320,000	202,878	443,000	312,315	–
160,000	103,215	235,000	166,365	2,081
35,000	10,311	41,000	17,185	346
20,000	11,153	27,000	18,588	3,160
425	110	725	184	14
215,425	124,789	303,725	202,322	5,601
–	–	–	–	0
–	–	–	–	0
4,800	3,600	6,300	5,100	(79)
–	–	–	–	0
–	–	10,000	9,000	27
1,500	2,125	2,000	2,625	(3,665)
1,700	1,000	2,200	1,500	(386)
–	–	–	–	(626)
836	834	993	991	(3,533)
-	–	–	–	(1,520)
8,000	8,000	8,000	8,000	(425)
1,000	973	2,000	1,946	330
5,000	4,059	5,000	4,059	(0)
10,000	10,000	10,000	10,000	(2,505)
7,500	5,000	10,000	7,500	1,022
15,000	10,451	15,000	10,451	0
7,500	5,584	10,000	8,084	51
62,836	51,626	81,493	69,256	(11,309)
278,261	176,416	385,218	271,579	(5,707)
41,739	26,462	57,783	40,737	(8,243)
320,000	202,878	443,000	312,315	(13,951)
(0)	–	(0)	–	(13,951)

① Currently, the support group activity of DV is funded by two foundation grants.

② This report shows any funding gaps—areas where grants do not cover costs. In this case, the Belle Foundation grant does not pay anything toward conference and meeting costs.

③ In some budgets, common costs are not allocated below-the-line. This is because in budgets prepared for funders, common costs are not presented any differently than the specific costs of executing an activity.

④ Administrative costs *are* allocated below the line. DV needs to know internally how much of its administrative costs each activity must bear.

A second thing to notice is that on this report, administrative costs are allocated below the line. Again, this is not something that DV does for its internal statements. But for the purposes of maximum cost recovery from funders, DV does need to see how much of its administrative costs each activity must bear. The primary way that DV recovers its administrative costs is by including a portion of them in each grant and contract budget submitted for a program activity. Funders expect to make a contribution to administration this way, and usually use the terms "overhead" or "indirect" to refer to these costs. This approach allows DV to recognize that the support groups activity needs to raise $447,947—not only its own costs of $384,927—in order to sustain DV's administrative activities.

Are we recovering costs from our key funders?

A directly related assessment question is how well the organization is recovering costs from its key funders. This is the nonprofit version of "pricing." In fact, there is a continuum of nonprofit pricing across organizational types. When an independent nonprofit school determines what its annual tuition will be, it behaves in a very similar fashion to a for-profit setting the price for its services: it determines the cost of providing the services, investigates what the market will pay, and sets the price. Less obviously, a nonprofit prices its programs every time it submits a foundation grant proposal budget or a government contract budget. One of the common ways that nonprofit businesses struggle financially is in unwittingly underpricing their programs—usually because they have inaccurately assessed the true costs of providing services.

It is a good idea to develop and regularly monitor Activity by Funding Source reports as a means of evaluating how effectively the organization is recovering its costs. Look at the Activity by Funding Sources report (Figure 14) for DV's support group activity. Currently this activity is supported by two foundation grants, but these two grants do not cover the full costs of the program. Note that the Belle Foundation does not cover any of the conference and meeting costs. This could be because these costs were for some reason excluded from the grant proposal budget submitted to them (and thus never approved), or perhaps the Belle Foundation has a policy about not paying for meeting expenses. Whatever the reason, it is important to identify the funding gaps in any program. Seeing these gaps clearly on an Activity by Funding Source report allows leadership to consider a number of courses of action, including renegotiation of grant and contract budgets, intentional inclusion of certain uncovered costs in future proposal budgets, adding earned income strategies, or containment of uncovered costs until additional funding can be identified.

Do we have a sustainable portfolio of activities?

Again, a nonprofit's activities are interdependent and the mix, or "portfolio" of activities, is a strategic consideration. The matrix in Figure 15 can help organizations assess their current portfolio of activities. Adapted from the Growth-Share Matrix developed by the Boston Consulting Group, it asks a leadership team to assess each of its core activities along two axes: mission accomplishment and financial sustainability. From a long-term financial health perspective, this assessment exercise is intended to clarify what is most important to the organization as well as what is most sustainable over time. There are four quadrants in the matrix:

1. STAR—High Mission Impact and High Sustainability: Keep and strengthen these activities.

2. HEART—High Mission Impact and Low Sustainability: Keep and build the sustainability of these activities.

3. MONEY SIGN—High Sustainability and Low Mission Impact: Keep and increase the mission impact of these activities.

4. STOP SIGN—Low Sustainability and Low Mission Impact: Close or transfer these activities.

Figure 15. Dual Bottom-Line Matrix

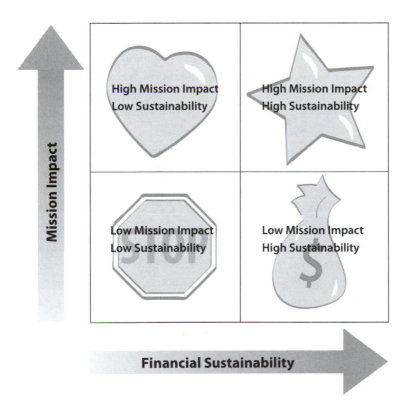

A team of organizational leaders candidly evaluates each activity (including fundraising activities) using historical financial data, knowledge of upcoming funding trends, and a thoughtful review of the organization's mission and values. Each activity is then plotted on the matrix. The matrix is called "Dual Bottom-Line" in reference to the two business objectives in play at a nonprofit business: accomplishing mission and financial health.[3]

Over time, many nonprofit businesses grow and change in ways that are not fundamentally aligned with their core purpose or financially sustainable. And yet because valuable staff people are running these efforts and because they provide some benefit to the organization's constituency, such programs get maintained and subsidized. It takes real financial leadership to look beyond the potential short-term hardship of closing a program to the long-term benefit that closure could bring to the organization. Even if you are not in a position to close or give away programs (though this is not considered often enough in nonprofits), the process of putting each program through this kind of assessment will inform your financial planning and fundraising strategy. Moreover, in leading your team through this exercise, you model the leadership principle of fostering a mission and money culture at your organization.

In DV's case, the shelter program is completely aligned with its founding purpose of providing a safe place for domestic violence survivors and their children to live temporarily, so the activity is placed at the highest point on the mission axis. While the shelter program does have a large government contract, it does not fully cover the program's costs, so the activity is placed three quarters of the way up the sustainability axis. It is a "star" program that needs a bit of improvement in the sustainability arena. The support groups are viewed as a valuable program but not as core to DV's mission, thus their lower placement than shelter services on the mission axis. In other words, should they become financially unsustainable, board and staff would be more comfortable cutting out the support groups than the shelter services. Over time, the board and management team would like the support groups to move into the star category—that is, to do a better job of covering their costs. DV's annual event is a moneymaker, which staff should strive to make as mission-relevant as possible—perhaps by including former clients as speakers during the program or inserting fact sheets about domestic violence in the invitations. Some board members are contemplating adding an additional moneymaker to the portfolio—perhaps a golf tournament—to generate unrestricted funds that compensate for the financial performance of the core programs.

As a nonprofit grows over time, the matrix can get very crowded, which requires staff and board to be honest and disciplined in their evaluation of each activity relative to the others. In facilitating this exercise with more complex

It takes real financial leadership to look beyond the potential short-term hardship of closing a program to the long-term benefit that closure could bring to the organization.

---

[3] For more on using this tool in organizational planning, please see *Strategic Planning for Nonprofit Organizations: A Practical Guide and Workbook*, by CompassPoint staff Mike Allison and Jude Kaye, published by John Wiley and Sons, Inc.

Figure 16. DV's Dual Bottom-Line Matrix

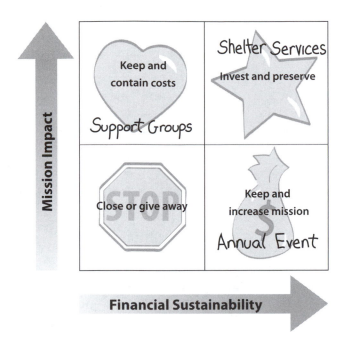

organizations than DV, we have found two potential challenges. First, when management staff is invested in preserving the jobs of the people they supervise, it can be difficult for them to speak candidly about the relatively low impact some activities have on the organization's mission. Second, funding cuts on the immediate horizon may cause the leadership team to dismiss an activity as unsustainable when in fact new or different sources might be available. The financial leader should ensure a thorough evaluation of each activity's current and potential status if the dual bottom-line analysis is employed.

Are our income streams stable and sufficiently diverse?

It is extremely important to take a multiyear perspective in your assessment of income trends at your organization. A multiyear historical analysis combined with current data gathering about likely shifts in the priorities or giving power of your key donor groups can illuminate important data for your planning process. Let's use DV to see how to conduct such an assessment. Figure 17, DV's Income Trend Analysis, is a report that shows income totals by DV's major types of funding over the last two years as well as a projection through this year-end. This presentation engages key staff and board in a discussion of the factors contributing to the trends in each case.

Figure 17. Income Trend Analysis

Domestic Violence Intervention & Prevention Agency
Income Trend Analysis
As of March 31, 2005

Funding Source	Actual 2002–03 $	Actual 2002–03 %	Actual 2003–04 $	Actual 2003–04 %	Forecast 2004–05 $	Forecast 2004–05 %
Annual campaign	29,565	2.30%	19,385	1.40%	15,000	0.90%
Major gifts	19,750	1.60%	22,500	1.60%	18,000	1.10%
Board donations	18,750	1.50%	21,250	1.50%	25,000	1.50%
Events (net)	90,430	7.10%	104,880	7.30%	125,000	7.60%
Endowment	–	0.00%	100,000	7.00%	10,000	0.60%
Foundation grants - unrestricted	22,500	1.80%	12,750	0.90%	115,000	7.00%
Foundation grants - temp. restricted ❶	439,000	34.60%	439,000	30.80%	550,000	33.70%
Government contracts ❷	644,618	50.80%	710,698	49.80%	770,467	47.10%
Interest/dividends	5,204	0.40%	4,869	0.30%	5,750	0.40%
Investments	–	0.00%	(8,246)	-0.60%	–	0.00%
Total income	1,269,817	100.00%	1,427,086	100.00%	1,634,217	100.00%
Net assets released from restriction	387,541		570,746		453,000	

❶ While DV has ten different types of income (income streams), the vast majority of dollars reside in two categories: Foundation grants - temporarily restricted and Government contracts.

❷ DV's Government Contract income is in the form of one large state contract, thus its diversification *within* this type of income is weak.

In forecasting income, DV relies on data it has internally as well as external data such as informal discussions with funders, news and gossip from peer organizations, and stock market and giving trends reported in the media. If a financial leader is not assessing income trends, she or he may miss some fairly obvious "writing on the wall" and continue to plan based on outdated assumptions. In any business—nonprofit or otherwise—this can lead to disaster.

As you are analyzing income trends by type, consider the diversification of your income streams. It stands to reason that a nonprofit business that depends on a single source of funding—be it a major donor, a foundation grant, or a government contract—for 50 percent of its funding, is in an extremely vulnerable position should that funding source cease to exist, shift its funding priorities, or significantly reduce its annual award. In the challenging economy of the last several years, nonprofit leaders have become even more aware of the value of income diversification. Think of diversification in two ways: across income streams and within income streams.

Diversification across income streams means generating income from a variety of types of sources: individuals, corporations, foundations, government agencies, and so on. This is critical because these sources tend to give different types of funding; individuals typically give unrestricted support, while most foundations invest in a specific program or activity. You may need a mix of these to ensure flexibility in spending, cover full activity costs, and to build a reserve.

Diversification within income streams means having a variety of donors or funders within each funding type; that is, one hundred individual donors rather than just five; and four foundation funders rather than one. Again, the less reliant a nonprofit is on any one source, the more readily it can financially absorb the loss of a source. To determine the degree of income diversification at DV, look at the simple analysis on page 54. This trend analysis is easily prepared by a development assistant or a bookkeeper and facilitates the financial leaders' monitoring of diversification over time.

At DV, such analysis demonstrated that while DV has done a good job of attracting different types of funding, within some funding types it is reliant on a single or handful of sources. For instance, its government funding comes in the form of one large state contract for its shelter activity. This leaves DV very vulnerable to the political decisions made by those who hold the purse strings. There may or may not be other available government funds for the shelter, but this analysis should inspire the leader to find out. At the very least, it reminds staff and board of how critical it is to maintain a strong relationship with this government funder, including meeting or surpassing service goals and staying in touch with the individual decision makers at the government agency.

Diversification *across* income streams means generating income from a variety of types of sources. Diversification *within* income streams means having a variety of donors or funders within each funding type.

3. Do our constituents perceive us as efficient and competitive?

Here you are considering how your constituents, funders, watchdog groups, the media, and the like may perceive your organization externally. The questions a financial leader should be able to answer include:

- Do we have enough cash and receivables to match our temporarily restricted net assets—or commitments to spend according to donor intent?
- Are we releasing funds from restriction—or fulfilling commitments according to donor intent—as we had planned?
- Is our overhead rate appropriate?
- Are our fundraising efforts cost-effective?
- Is our cost per mission output/outcome competitive?

Do we have enough cash and receivables to match our temporarily restricted net assets—or commitments to spend according to donor intent?

We have talked in several places in this book about the importance of managing restricted contributions well. Both the executive director and key board members should be assessing the organization's management of restricted funds on a regular basis to avoid inadvertently misappropriating these funds. Common ways that nonprofit organizations get in trouble with restricted funds include using restricted funds to cover unallowable costs, and raising more restricted money than the organization can actually spend in the grant period on the approved activities.

One way to assess whether your organization is managing restricted contributions well is to look at the Statement of Financial Position and do a quick comparison between your current cash and receivables total and the total restricted net assets reported. If you don't have as much cash on hand or on the way (receivables) as you have restricted net assets, then the organization may have spent funds in unapproved ways and could have insufficient funds to meet its commitment to funders. In other words, you want to confirm that the organization has enough money to spend in the way it promised its funders it would. Look at DV's Statement of Financial Position (Figure 11) to see that DV's total cash and receivables are slightly more than their temporarily restricted net assets.

Are we releasing funds from restriction—or fulfilling commitments according to donor intent—as we had planned?

Another indicator to watch in the arena of managing restricted funds is planning for their release from restriction. Release is the financial term for meeting the commitments made to the funder. In financial terms, the way that a nonprofit fulfills its commitment to funders is by spending money in the manner it said it would in the approved grant or donation budget. Each month as funds are spent appropriately, they are released from restriction to cover these appropriate expenses.

Note that on DV's Budgeted Statement of Activities (Figure 12), "net assets released from restriction" are the last type of income listed in the first column of the statement. Additional detail is found in Figure 18, DV's Restricted Funds Detail report, which is maintained by DV's Financial Manager.

In a sense, a nonprofit looks to its own holdings of restricted funds as an income stream to cover its expenses. As such, it should actually plan for—or budget for—the release of its restricted funds. In doing so, it asks the question, "When will we be able to fulfill this commitment to spend funds as promised

Figure 18. DV Restricted Funds Detail

Domestic Violence Intervention & Prevention Agency
2004–05 Restricted Funds Detail
As of March 31, 2005

Funder	Purpose	Beginning Balance	This Year Raised	This Year Released	Remaining	Future Years	Ending Balance
Allen Foundation	Support Groups	–	266,000	109,437	13,563	143,000	156,563
Belle Foundation	Support Groups	300,000	150,000	202,878	117,122	130,000	247,122
Community Foundation	Fundraising Planning	26,004	–	10,020	–	15,984	15,984
Total		326,004	416,000	322,335	130,685	288,984	419,669

to this funder?" Thus, release of restricted funds becomes an assessment issue for the financial leader, who must monitor if in fact the nonprofit is releasing those funds as it had planned. For instance, if a nonprofit is far behind where it planned to be in releasing funds from restriction, it may mean that it has hit unexpected roadblocks in a funded program, such as the inability to hire a program manager or a serious lack of demand from constituents. So, the inability to spend money as planned may mean that there are programmatic problems that need to be surfaced and solved.

In DV's case, the organization is behind schedule in releasing funds from restriction. In other words, DV is using up its restricted funds more slowly than it expected, which could mean that DV will have ultimately fewer resources available this year than it initially projected. It also means that some funders may need notifying of DV's inability to meet programmatic outcomes.

Is our overhead rate appropriate?

There are a variety of ways that donors and funders evaluate whether or not to support a nonprofit organization. Increasingly a key indicator they use is the degree to which a contribution is directed to program activities versus overhead activities. Rightfully, donors want to feel confident that the majority of their contribution is enabling mission accomplishment directly (except in the case of specific infrastructure investments by funders). Aside from donor perceptions, as the financial leader, you want to ensure that spending on overhead is not excessive, because it is part of your commitment to all of your organization's stakeholders to accomplish as much good work on their behalf as you can with your limited resources. So it is critical that leadership monitors how the organization is performing in this arena.

The Better Business Bureau's Wise Giving Alliance (www.give.org) recommends that nonprofits not spend more than $.35 of every $1 on overhead. Total overhead costs are calculated by adding administration and fundraising costs. Look at DV's Statement of Activities (Figure 5) to find these costs:

Overhead Ratio:
Admin. + Fundraising
————————————
Total Expenses

$$\frac{\text{Administration + Fundraising } (\$167,183 + 163,763) = \quad \$330,946}{\text{Total Expenses} \qquad\qquad\qquad\qquad\qquad = \$1,114,050} = 30\%$$

When you compare overhead costs to total expenses, DV has an overhead rate of 30 percent. In other words, of every dollar DV spends, 30 cents is spent on administration and fundraising, and 70 cents is spent on the direct costs of delivering its services. Nonprofit organizations will vary in their overhead costs; there is no "right answer" here. Consider how legitimately different the overhead percentages can be across organizations. A nonprofit human service organization that receives 90 percent of its funding from government sources is likely to have a much lower overhead percentage than an advocacy organization with no government support. Why? Because the advocacy nonprofit has to spend considerable time and expense cultivating donors through the mail, Internet, and events—expensive activities that can have modest yields—whereas the human service agency gets the vast majority of its funding from a handful of large contracts and thus spends next to nothing on fundraising.

Remember that we established a financial leadership foundational principle in Chapter 1 that investing in infrastructure is a worthy financial decision. Indeed, in assessing your organization's overhead percentage, it would be a mistake to say, "the lower the better." On the contrary, a healthy, but not excessive investment in overhead leads to more productive and efficient organizations properly equipped to grow and thrive. And a final reminder about your assessment of overhead: It is rather common among undertrained finance bookkeepers to be unaware of the necessity of tracking overhead costs separately throughout the year. As we argued in Chapter 2, if the bookkeeper does not know nonprofit accounting, it's your role as the financial leader to invest in his or her professional development so that you can confidently use your financial statements for assessment.

Are our fundraising efforts cost-effective?

Since fundraising is so central to the long-term survival of the majority of nonprofit businesses, the question of what kind of financial return an organization is getting for its fundraising efforts is another critical efficiency measure. Effective leaders set clear financial targets for each of their fundraising strategies (events, grants, annual campaign to individual donors, and so forth) and the fundraising effort overall. Too often nonprofits proceed with inefficient fundraising strategies, because they are traditions or because nobody analyzes their return to reveal the inefficiencies. Staff and volunteers may focus too much on the impressive-sounding gross of a fundraising activity rather than its net financial return after expenses.

To calculate return, compare the costs of raising contributions with the total contributions raised. So if a nonprofit spends $5,000 to raise $25,000, its fundraising return would be 5:1. In other words, for every dollar it spends on fundraising, it receives $5 in contributions. Optimum return will vary by fundraising strategy. For instance, it might cost $5,000 worth of a grantwriter's time to draft a winning grant proposal that brings in a $125,000 award—a return of 25:1. In contrast, the cost to write, design, print, and mail a newsletter that includes a donation envelope might be $25,000 and yield just $40,000 in contributions—a return of 1.6:1. Of course, the organization likely has other goals for the newsletter in addition to fundraising, so a relatively modest fundraising return may be acceptable. Setting clear goals for fundraising return and monitoring these goals throughout the year is an important way for the executive director to support and evaluate fundraising staff or consultants.

A look at DV's Statement of Activities (Figure 5) will help us calculate the return of its fundraising program overall. By dividing its total contributions by its fundraising expenses, we create a ratio of contributed funds to fundraising costs.

$$\frac{\text{Total Support} = \$628,630}{\text{Total Fundraising Expense} = \$163,763} = \frac{3.84}{1}$$

This is a return of almost 4:1, which seems like a good investment.

If you are approaching fundraising return from the perspective of evaluating the efforts of your fundraising staff, you may need to calculate the ratio differently. If the fundraising staff has nothing to do with receipt of certain contributions, then including those funds in the calculation would overstate their personal results. We can recalculate the return—this time excluding restricted contributions, which are sometimes generated by program staff themselves. In this case, you are comparing just unrestricted support ($207,630) to total fundraising expenses ($163,763) and the return is a less impressive 1.27:1.

Determining which calculation (the one that includes all contributions or the one that excludes restricted contributions) is more useful depends on what kinds of contributions your fundraising staff or consultant is charged with raising. If program people manage their own grants and contracts while your development person is primarily responsible for unrestricted donations such as the annual campaign and an annual event, then the second calculation is a more fair assessment of your fundraising return. In any case, getting in the habit of tracking the fundraising return and reporting on it to key staff and board is an important facet of financial leadership.

Effective leaders set clear financial targets for each of their fundraising strategies (events, grants, annual campaign to individual donors) and the fundraising effort overall.

Fundraising Return Ratio:

$$\frac{\text{Total Support}}{\text{Total Fundraising Expense}}$$

Is our cost per mission output competitive?

Overhead is not the only area where good financial leadership calls for efficiency. You should also establish a way of assessing the cost of doing your mission-related work. This involves identifying what a "unit" or "output" of work is, given your organization's programs or activities. This is harder for some organizations than others. For instance, in DV's case, it is quite clear that there are two units of mission-related work: shelter nights provided and support group visits provided. On the other hand, an environmental advocacy organization may decide that its informational media campaigns—which may be varied in length and objectives—are the mission-related outputs.

Once these units are identified, you can analyze the cost of producing them. For instance, monitoring these costs will help you identify optimal program size given economies of scale; that is, how does cost per output change at different levels of program investment? Being able to describe costs in this way is also extremely valuable in fundraising; it allows you to make very real for potential donors what their funds will accomplish—that is, you want to say, "Your donation will provide forty-one shelter nights" rather than simply "Your donation will support shelter services."

In the health and human services arena, governments and foundations are increasingly thinking about the cost to meet broad social objectives—as opposed to the cost to maintain salaries and other fixed expenses. The focus is more and more on what it really costs to move an unemployed single mother into a living wage job, or reduce HIV infection rates among IV drug users in New York City. These are complex outcomes that may take multiple fiscal years for an organization to accomplish. Thus, the notion of trying to affix a specific price tag to them is challenging. More often, we focus on the cost of outputs—the job skills, workshops, and case management hours for the unemployed single mother, and the outreach hours and HIV testing for the IV drug users. The more you can talk in mission-related language about the way you use financial resources, the more competitive your organization will be.

If you are doing a good job of tracking expenses by core function (which was a key accounting concept introduced in Chapter 2), then calculating your cost per unit of program work should not be difficult. The program cost data will come right out of your accounting system. The other data you need is how many outputs you are generating, which in community-based organizations can sometimes be a bit more challenging. This is where program tracking and financial tracking can and should interface. Ensuring that your program staff are accurately tracking their accomplishments is part of your leadership role.

The more you can talk in mission-related language about the way you use financial resources, the more competitive your organization will be.

Let's look at the example of DV's cost per shelter night provided. On DV's Statement of Activities (Figure 5), find the total cost of shelter services. A program database supplies the number of shelter nights provided.

$$\frac{\text{Costs of Shelter Service with allocated costs} = \$505,874}{\text{Number of shelter nights provided} = 7,254} = \$69.74/\text{night}$$

> **Cost Per Service Unit:**
>
> Activity Costs
> (including all allocated costs)
> ──────────────────
> Service Units Provided

Comparing the cost per mission unit to other organizations doing similar work should be possible using the Form 990, for DV and for other organizations. These are in the searchable GuideStar online database at www.guidestar.org. Form 990 includes a requirement to break down program accomplishments and their costs. If this data is not available, talking to some of your core funders—who likely invest in other providers like you—can be a source of comparative information.

Evaluate Your Organization's Financial Health

Take the organizational evaluation in Figure 19 on pages 62–63 to consider the current financial health of your nonprofit. Elena's answers and comments are highlighted for your reference under "comments." A complete blank version of the evaluation tool can be found in Appendix B.

Summary

A nonprofit financial leader and his or her key partners on the board and staff need to be able to evaluate the financial strengths and weaknesses of the organization from a variety of perspectives. They should be constantly aware of the immediate financial issues facing the organization, such as cash flow challenges or major variances in income and spending compared with the year's budget. They should also look at trends and how well the organization is positioned to thrive in future years. And finally, they also have to assess perceived efficiency from the point of view of potential donors and funders, competitor organizations, and watchdog groups. All of this assessment work will inform the kinds of financial goals (budget and work plan) that a well-led organization sets for itself for the following year.

Chapter 3 helped you get a clear picture of your organization's current financial health. In Chapter 4, you will learn about financial planning for your organization—specifically, good processes that will translate the organization's goals and work plans into an accurate, useful budget.

Figure 19.   Financial Health Assessment

Category	Red	Yellow	Green	Comments	Action Plan
Current Ratio	Ratio of current assets to current liabilities is less than 1:1.	Ratio of current assets to current liabilities is between 1:1 and 3:1.	Ratio of current assets to current liabilities is greater than 3:1.	Overall liquidity is strength.	Monitor timing of government contract payments.
Cash Flow	Cash flow is a constant problem resulting in frequent delays in payroll and late fees from vendors.	We have occasional periods of cash flow challenge, which we weather by delaying select payments to vendors.	Cash flow is either not a challenge or the challenge is anticipated and managed by delaying large expenditures or use of a line of credit.	Certain periods of the year can be very tight.	Obtain line of credit.
Budget Variances	The organization has large variances between planned and actual income for the year to date, but continues to spend at the pace originally budgeted.	While there are some variances between planned and actual income for the year to date, we have reduced spending to maintain our planned year-end surplus/deficit.	We are on track with our financial plan for the year.	While we are close to being on track, we are not generating sufficient surplus on a year-to-year basis.	Plan for surplus in 05–06.
Cash Management	The finance manager leaves all idle cash in the operating checking account.	The finance manager moves idle cash to an interest-bearing account.	At the direction of the board finance committee, the finance manager pursues investment opportunities in line with the organization's documented Investment Policy.	Our cash resources are relatively small and easy to manage.	As we grow our endowment, we must develop investment policies.
Restricted Fund Balance	The organization has less cash and receivables than its total restricted net assets.	The organization has as much cash and receivables as it has total restricted net assets.	The organization has more cash and receivables than its total restricted net assets.	None	Continue to manage and monitor temporarily restricted funds.
Releases from Restriction	The organization does not budget for or routinely assess its release of funds from restriction.	The organization is behind its plan for the year in releasing funds from restriction.	The organization is meeting its goal for the year of releasing funds from restriction.	We need to do a better job at covering all support group program costs with our grants.	Eliminate support group reliance on unrestricted funds.
Overhead Rate	The organization has an overhead rate of less than 15% or more than 30%.	The organization has an overhead rate between 26% and 30%.	The organization has an overhead rate of between 15% and 25%.	Although we are doing well here, we'd like to dedicate more resources to core program areas.	Reduce overhead rate in 05–06.

Figure 19. Financial Health Assessment continued

Category	Red	Yellow	Green	Comments	Action Plan
Fundraising Effectiveness	The organization has no targets for fundraising return and never calculates it.	The organization maintains some fundraising efforts that are not cost-effective.	The organization ensures the cost-effectiveness of its fundraising efforts.	We have built development infrastructure and expect to see more dollars raised and effectiveness improve over time.	Improve fundraising effectiveness in O5–O6.
Cost per Unit	The organization has no targets for cost per unit and does not monitor it.	The organization has a cost per unit that is not competitive with other organizations doing similar work.	The organization has a cost per unit that is competitive with other organizations doing similar work.	None	Continue to monitor per unit costs.
Operating Reserve	The organization has an unrestricted reserve of less than one month's operating expenses.	The organization has an unrestricted reserve of between one and three month's operating expenses.	The organization has an unrestricted reserve of four to twelve month's operating expenses.	Our reserve is insufficient for our planned growth.	Improve reserve ratio in O5–O6.
Profit/Loss by Activity	The organization does not have financial data by activity, so it cannot determine how core programs are performing financially.	The organization is carrying multiple programs with significant operating deficits.	While some core programs run small deficits, management focuses on recovering all possible costs from key funders and raising unrestricted support for subsidization.	None	Eliminate support group reliance on unrestricted funds.
Program Portfolio	Leadership does not assess the sustainability of our mix of activities.	Based upon recent assessment, leadership is trying to shift the mission-impact and/or financial sustainability of some core activities.	The organization has a good portfolio of activities that together result in high mission impact and financial health.	We have built development infrastructure and expect to see more dollars raised and effectiveness improve over time.	Improve fundraising effectiveness in O5–O6.
Diversity of Funding	The organization is dependent on a handful of funding sources of a single type.	The organization relies on multiple funding sources across two types of funding.	The organization relies on many sources across three or more funding streams.	The shelter program is overly dependent on city funds.	Grow endowment to provide income in perpetuity for shelter.

4. Financial Planning

The next aspect of financial leadership is financial planning, which takes place largely through the annual budgeting process. An annual <u>budget</u> is the financial reflection of what a nonprofit business expects to accomplish over a twelve-month period. For many nonprofit executives, budgeting is the most comfortable and interesting part of financial leadership. Done correctly, the budgeting process actively engages many staff and board members who are uninterested in accounting or even monthly financial reporting. It becomes an opportunity for these stakeholders to contribute to the organization's work plan. For most organizations, the annual budgeting cycle also offers the best (if not only) time to set meaningful financial goals. As your organization's financial leader, you want to ensure that the process results in a useful tool—one that will be used to anticipate problems and to provide a baseline against which actual program and financial performance can be monitored. This chapter introduces the guiding principles of effective budgeting and then outlines the five steps to building a strong annual budget.

Guiding Principles of Effective Budgeting

In order to lead a successful annual budgeting process, a financial leader must embrace two fundamental budgeting principles: first, a budget is a tool for *planning* and *monitoring;* and second, a good budgeting process is *inclusive* of many voices and perspectives. Let's look at each of these principles more closely.

A tool for planning and monitoring

The process of building a budget is fundamentally a planning process. In fact, in the course of planning for its future, an organization will often revisit its purpose, mission, goals, objectives, strategies, and activities. This is a healthy and necessary time of annual reflection and one of the primary reasons that the budgeting process should begin several months before year-end. Even in a relatively straightforward budgeting process where there seems little doubt about the organization's overall direction, the act of determining what the organization wants to accomplish, how much that will cost, and how the necessary resources will be generated, is a form of strategic planning—if done thoughtfully.

Once adopted, the budget becomes an essential financial management tool that will be helpful in monitoring and controlling ongoing organization activities throughout the year. With each reporting cycle, the organization compares actual performance against its plan. If the organization has gone "off track," various responses can be considered. If, for example, a program is costing more than anticipated, it may be necessary for management to bring costs down through staff reductions or a freeze on non-personnel expenses. Or leadership may decide to revise the plan to take the higher level of expense into account. Using the budget as an ongoing monitoring tool raises these sorts of strategic discussions at the staff and board levels.

To summarize, in developing and actively monitoring a budget, nonprofits:

- Define organizational goals
- Outline the resource needs and uses to accomplish their goals
- Monitor progress throughout the time period
- Point out significant variances between the financial goals and how resources are actually being used
- Take corrective action as problems arise

An inclusive process

The second guiding principle of budgeting is that to be accurate, effective, and uniting, *the budgeting process must be inclusive*. While the executive director and key finance staff will play the coordinating role in the process, all management and board members have a role to play. Unfortunately, for many nonprofit organizations, planning and financial management are activities that divide rather than unite the organization. Program planners and fiscal managers speak different languages and often have different priorities; they may or may not be aware of the importance of each other's approach to the budget process. Program planning decisions often are viewed as failing to reflect economic realities, while fiscal management decisions are often viewed as insensitive to the programmatic mission of the organization. These conflicts are often fought out during the budgeting process—the very process that could unite these viewpoints. The leadership challenge is to insist that these various perspectives are heard and considered by all parties with the collective goal of developing a realistic and inspiring plan for the coming year.

So what roles do all the players have in an inclusive budgeting process? Board members provide big picture direction and oversight to the process; they also vet and ultimately approve the final budget. Program managers plan for the costs needed to accomplish their program objectives; in some cases, they are also the best people to plan for program-generated income. Development staff plan for the contributed income that can realistically be included in the budget as well as the costs they will incur to raise it. The finance manager serves as <u>budget manager</u> during the process: collecting input, building the Excel budget workbook, and updating and distributing drafts. Finance staff also plan for the organization's administrative and common costs. Through it all, the executive director is akin to a symphony conductor, providing overall strategic direction and challenging staff to be both creative and disciplined in their planning. In the best-case scenario, building the budget is truly a team effort.

To be sure, an inclusive process can be a messy one with a great deal of debate and even frustration at times, but one of the financial leadership principles we outlined in Chapter 1 is that a financial leader wants company. The budgeting process is the ideal time each year to bring an organizational cross-section into the financial leadership effort. The executive director who creates the budget during an all-nighter before the first board meeting of the year (or asks his or her finance manager to do so) is almost guaranteeing a less-than-accurate plan and a useless tool for controlling financial activity throughout the year. Remember that it is human nature to respond to and feel accountable to a plan you developed. In our consulting work with nonprofits, we do not see leaders having much luck holding program and development staff accountable to budgets they did not contribute to meaningfully.

Building the Annual Budget

There are five stages of the budgeting process:

1. Defining the planning context and goals
2. Estimating costs
3. Forecasting income
4. Striking the balance between goals and resources
5. Approving the plan

Depending on the size and complexity of the organization, the entire budget building process may require two to four months. The staff person acting as budget manager should create and distribute a budget calendar with time frames and assignments of responsibilities for each activity. For a midsized organization with a fiscal year beginning on July 1, the budget calendar might look like that shown in Figure 21, Budget Calendar, page 68.

**Figure 20.
Budgeting Process**

1. Define planning context and goals

2. Estimate costs

3. Forecast income

4. Strike the balance

5. Approve the plan

Figure 21. Budget Calendar

April	• Board and staff retreat to review performance and develop annual goals
	• Program coordinators establish program plan and estimate "direct" program costs
May	• Finance manager and executive director estimate common and administrative costs
	• Fundraising team creates income plan and estimates fundraising costs
	• Management team creates capital budget needed to support program, administrative, and fundraising plans
June	• Finance manager prepares annual cash flow projection
	• Management team and finance committee adjust income and expenses, as needed
	• Full board approves final budget
July	• Management team implements annual plan and budget
	• Evaluate budgeting process
October	• First Quarter budget review
January	• Midyear budget review (and revision, if needed)
April	• Third Quarter budget review
	• Begin budget planning for new fiscal year
Ongoing	• Monthly review of actual results to program plan and budget

In DV's case, the budgeting process begins with the budget calendar. The calendar is developed working backwards from the last board meeting of the fiscal year (June). The finance committee meets twice in the month before the board meeting (May)—once to review and give feedback on the first draft, and once to approve the revised draft. Each member of the management team uses worksheets prepared by the finance director (which include the year-to-date actuals versus last year's budget) to contribute to the first draft: The director of programs prepares the program cost estimate and projects revenue from government contracts; the development director forecasts individual donations and corporate and foundation support; and the finance director prepares the administrative cost estimate, the common cost allocation, the capital budget, and the investment income forecast.

Using DV's planning cycle and story, let's look more closely at each of the five stages in an effective budgeting process.

1. Defining the planning context and goals

Budgeting for the upcoming year should not be seen as "starting over" with a blank slate. In fact, a lot of strategic thinking and reflection should happen before you begin the process of identifying specific income and expense targets. By "define the planning context," we mean that a budget does not exist in a vacuum. Instead it should respond specifically to the organization's current operating context. Therefore, a thorough assessment of your organization's financial strengths and weaknesses (as outlined in Chapter 3) is a critical aspect of this preparatory work. Which financial weaknesses will the organization try to address in the coming year? As part of defining the planning context, you will also want to look closely at what the organization accomplished programmatically over the past year. What does the organization want to do differently or better next year?

A second dimension of the planning context is *external*. The management team should scan environmental opportunities and threats. Typical opportunities that face nonprofit businesses include: expansion of a program into a new geographic area; partnership with another nonprofit to improve services or impact; initiation of a capital campaign; and pursuit of a new funding stream. Typical threats include: the loss of a major funding source; a new competitor in your mission area; and unfavorable political changes at the local, state, or national levels. The management team should assign data-gathering to each of its members and hold a special session to report back on and consider external environmental factors that will influence planning.

Together, these strengths, weaknesses, opportunities, and threats become the assumptions to which your planning process will respond. At DV, defining the planning context resulted in board and management setting three overarching goals for 2005–06. First, to remain competitive, they want to prioritize program stability and quality. They will accomplish this by investing in more competitive compensation for staff, updating technology for the programs, and adding more direct client financial support—which the program managers have identified as critical to successful client outcomes. Second, they want to improve on some of DV's "yellow" and "red" financial health and efficiency indicators: grow the reserve, lower their overhead rate, and establish a line of credit to manage cash flow challenges. And third, DV's leadership wants to improve fundraising effectiveness: grow the endowment, engage board members in giving, increase the pipeline of restricted contributions, and achieve better cost-recovery (including common and administrative costs) from major sources. Figure 22, DV's 2005–06 Budget Goals and Objectives, reflects these aims.

With these goals articulated early in the process, managers have a clear understanding of what the organization overall is trying to accomplish. This in turn will help them make better planning decisions at the level of their individual programs or departments. In short, they are positioned to make more strategic choices as the organization moves into the expense and income forecasting stages of the process.

By articulating goals early in the process, managers can make better planning decisions.

Figure 22. 2005–06 Budget: Goals and Objectives

Domestic Violence Intervention & Prevention Agency
2005–06 Budget: Goals and Objectives ❶
As of April 15, 2005

Overall Goal	2005–06 Objective
Stabilize programs and ensure highest quality	Salary increases to all staff
	Replace computers and equipment
	Increase direct client support
Improve on key financial health indicators ❷	Build liquid operating reserve
	Reduce overhead rate
	Obtain line of credit
Maximize fundraising effectiveness	Increase endowment income
	Increase board role in fundraising
	Build temporarily restricted balance
	Maximize cost recovery in foundation grants

❶ The culmination of step one of the budgeting process, this document is created by board and staff *before* staff begin estimating costs. Staff respond to these goals as they forecast expense and income during the budgeting process.

❷ These goals respond to the financial assessment described in Chapter 3.

2. Estimating costs

Expenses are the reflection of the work the organization wants to get done. A budgeting process that is motivated by quality programming and mission impact requires that the first round of expense forecasting be done *independently* from the first round of income forecasting. If the management team limits itself to considering only work that's currently funded, an important planning opportunity is missed. Certainly in stage four of the budgeting process (Striking the Balance) pragmatism will rear its head, but for now leadership should encourage managers to think about how best to accomplish mission next year.

When estimating the organization's expenses, you will be considering specific activity costs and common costs that every activity has to bear, as well as any capital expenditures necessary to support the organization's goals. In budgeting, it is helpful to think of administration and fundraising as activities just like program activities: they have expenses and income that need to be forecast. Program, development, and finance managers are usually in the best position to estimate the specific costs associated with their plans for the year. Based on past experience and current goals, the organization's managers should determine the number of staff members, supplies, and other resources needed to attain their objectives. When historical reference information is lacking or incomplete, it may be helpful to call on the experiences of your peers at similar organizations.

Also, remember that some costs are more hidden than others. For example, if a new program will require ten new staff positions, the expense estimates must also include time to hire, train, and support the new staff, as well as additional benefits, advertising costs, office equipment, and so forth. If a program is going to cut staff, there may be attendant costs such as outplacement, severance packages, and unemployment compensation. An experienced finance manager acting in the role of budget manager can help less experienced program and development managers anticipate these hidden costs.

Expenses are the reflection of the work the organization wants to get done.

We've broken the expenses you need to estimate out into four types:

- Personnel costs

- Activity-specific costs

- Full activity costs

- Capital acquisitions

Let's look at each in turn.

Estimating personnel costs

As personnel costs are typically the largest expense in a nonprofit's business, and because full-time equivalents (FTE) per activity is a driver of common cost allocation, it makes sense to start the cost estimation process with personnel. Figures 23 and 24, DV Staffing Plan, shows DV's personnel worksheet; in it, you can see the actual staff used to provide services and the requisite amount of each person's time. In response to DV's goal of decreasing overhead expenses, the staffing level budgeted for administration and development in 2005–06 is actually lower than the current staffing pattern (04–05).

Figure 23. 2005–06 Budget: Staffing Plan – FTE

Domestic Violence Intervention & Prevention Agency
2005–06 Budget: Staffing Plan – FTE
As of April 22, 2005

Name	Position	2005–06 Total	Shelter Services	Support Groups	Admin.	Fund-raising	Common Costs	❸ 2004–05 Total
Elena	Executive Director ❶	1.00	0.10	0.25	0.40	0.25	–	1.00
Freda	Director of Finance and Admin.	0.75	–	–	0.75	–	–	1.00
Albert	Accounting Manager	0.50	–	–	0.50	–	–	0.50
Ina	IT Manager	0.50	–	–	–	–	0.50	0.50
Ollie	Office Manager	1.00	–	–	–	–	1.00	1.00
Carla	Custodian	0.50	–	–	–	–	0.50	0.50
Paula	Director of Programs	1.00	0.60	0.40	–	–	–	1.00
Sherri	Shelter Manager	1.00	1.00	–	–	–	–	1.00
Denise	Day Coordinator	1.00	1.00	–	–	–	–	1.00
Natalie	Night Coordinator	1.00	1.00	–	–	–	–	1.00
India	Intake Coordinator	1.00	1.00	–	–	–	–	1.00
Cathy	Caseworker	1.00	1.00	–	–	–	–	1.00
Connie	Counselor	1.00	1.00	–	–	–	–	1.00
Alexis	Advocacy Manager	1.00	–	1.00	–	–	–	1.00
Adriana	Adult Community Organizer	1.00	–	1.00	–	–	–	1.00
Yani	Youth Community Organizer	1.00	–	1.00	–	–	–	1.00
Lani	Legislative Advocate	1.00	–	1.00	–	–	–	1.00
Dana	Director of Development	1.00	–	–	–	1.00	–	1.00
Dennis	Development Associate	0.75	–	–	–	0.75	–	1.00
		17.00	6.70	4.65	1.65	2.00	2.00	17.50
FTEs without common costs		15.00	6.70	4.65	1.65	2.00	(2.00)	
% of FTEs for allocation of common costs		100%	45%	31%	11%	13%	-100%	

❶ Notice that the executive director's FTE is split across all of DV's activities based on how she plans to spend her time over the coming year.

❷ Percentage of FTE for each activity. This percentage will be used to calculate common cost allocations.

❸ The budget manager includes last year's FTEs for comparison. DV is planning to decrease its FTE in 05–06 from 17.5 to 17.0.

Figure 24. 2005–06 Budget: Staffing Plan – Salaries

Domestic Violence Intervention & Prevention Agency
2005–06 Budget: Staffing Plan – Salaries
As of April 22, 2005

Name	Position	Salary (FTE)	Total FTE	Salary (adj)	Shelter Services	Support Groups	Admin.	Fund-raising	Common Costs
Elena	Executive Director	85,000	1.00	85,000	8,500	21,250	34,000	21,250	–
Freda	Director, Finance and Admin.	64,000	0.75	48,000	–	–	48,000	–	–
Albert	Accounting Manager	48,000	0.50	24,000	–	–	24,000	–	–
Ina	IT Manager	72,800	0.50	36,400	–	–	–	–	36,400
Ollie	Office Manager	38,000	1.00	38,000	–	–	–	–	38,000
Carla	Custodian	29,120	0.50	14,560	–	–	–	–	14,560
Paula	Director of Programs	58,000	1.00	58,000	34,800	23,200	–	–	–
Sherri	Shelter Manager	42,500	1.00	42,500	42,500	–	–	–	–
Denise	Day Coordinator	36,500	1.00	36,500	36,500	–	–	–	–
Natalie	Night Coordinator	37,200	1.00	37,200	37,200	–	–	–	–
India	Intake Coordinator	36,000	1.00	36,000	36,000	–	–	–	–
Cathy	Caseworker	38,500	1.00	38,500	38,500	–	–	–	–
Connie	Counselor	40,000	1.00	40,000	40,000	–	–	–	–
Alexis	Advocacy Manager	41,000	1.00	41,000	–	41,000	–	–	–
Adriana	Adult Community Organizer	35,250	1.00	35,250	–	35,250	–	–	–
Yani	Youth Community Organizer	35,750	1.00	35,750	–	35,750	–	–	–
Lani	Legislative Advocate	38,000	1.00	38,000	–	38,000	–	–	–
Dana	Director of Development	65,000	1.00	65,000	–	–	–	65,000	–
Dennis	Development Associate	39,000	0.75	29,250	–	–	–	29,250	–
All	Salary Increases ❷	8%		62,313	21,920	15,556	8,480	9,240	7,117
	Total		17.00	841,223	295,920	210,006	114,480	124,740	96,077

❶ This report is similar to Figure 23, but now actual salary dollars are spread by activity.

❷ At this stage, it is easier to work with salary increases in one lump percentage rather than by position.

Estimating activity-specific costs

Once the personnel worksheet is drafted, each activity manager can begin to work on his or her portion of the budget, which will include the key activity deliverables and estimates of the activity's specific costs. Based on the personnel worksheet and her plans for the program, Sherri, the DV shelter manager, estimated the shelter's volume of activity and its specific costs—reducing these to a final "cost per night" ratio, shown in Figure 25, DV Shelter Program Direct Costs (see below). Notice that at this stage, Sherri is considering two levels of activity: preserving core services and expansion of services (labeled "Core" and "Expanded" in the figures below). Remember, early in the process, Elena is encouraging her to think creatively about how DV could improve its shelter services. You can see that what Sherri wants to grow is direct client assistance (from the current level of $250,000 up to $375,000)—the financial and other resources they provide to women leaving batterers.

Estimating full activity costs

Even with personnel costs and other costs such as supplies included, the activity cost estimate is not complete. In estimating the cost of required resources, any organization with more than one activity must also determine the allocable portion of common costs, such as rent, telephone, utilities, and general supplies. For the purposes of identifying how much the program will try to recover from its funding sources, the organization may also want to determine each activity's allocable portion of administrative costs, such as accounting, office management, and general executive oversight. Without the *full* cost to execute a program (including common and administrative costs), staff will be unable to ensure cost-recovery in their fundraising efforts.

Given that one of DV's goals for the year is to maximize cost recovery from funders, both common and administrative costs are allocated to the shelter program. In Figure 26, page 76, notice how the percentage of program direct costs is used to determine how much of the organization's administrative costs to allocate to the shelter program. In other words, because DV spends 57.14 percent of its program dollars on the shelter program, the shelter program will be allocated 57.14 percent of DV's administrative costs. As Figure 26 shows, these costs add significantly to the cost per unit of service (night in the shelter).

Without the *full* cost to execute a program (including common and administrative costs), staff will be unable to ensure cost-recovery in their fundraising efforts.

Figure 25. 2005–06 Budget: Shelter Program Direct Costs

Domestic Violence Intervention & Prevention Agency
2005–06 Budget: Shelter Program Direct Costs
As of April 29, 2005

	Core	Expanded
Executive Director	8,500	8,500
Director of Programs	34,800	34,800
Shelter Manager	42,500	42,500
Day Coordinator	36,500	36,500
Night Coordinator	37,200	37,200
Intake Coordinator	36,000	36,000
Caseworker	38,500	38,500
Counselor	40,000	40,000
Salary increases	21,920	21,920
Salaries	295,920	295,920
Payroll taxes	30,332	30,332
Training	3,600	3,600
Personnel expenses	329,852	329,852
Clients, direct assistance to	250,000	375,000
Conferences and meetings	1,000	1,000
Dues and subscriptions	1,000	1,000
Other professional fees	20,000	20,000
Printing and copying	1,000	1,000
Supplies	15,000	15,000
Travel	3,750	3,750
Non-personnel expenses	291,750	416,750
Total specific costs	621,602	746,602
Shelter Nights		
Single Women	2,190	2,190
Women with Children	4,380	4,380
Infants/Toddlers	1,095	1,095
Children (2–12)	1,460	1,460
Teens (13–18)	730	730
Total Number of Nights	9,855	9,855
Cost per night ❸	$63.07	$75.76

❶ The shelter manager is considering two levels of activity. The Core column preserves services. The Expanded column adds services.

❷ The Expanded column reflects managers' thinking about ways to improve their programs next year. In this case, the program manager would like to increase direct client assistance.

❸ Note the cost per night when only direct program costs are included.

Figure 26. 2005–06 Budget: Shelter Program Full Costs

Domestic Violence Intervention & Prevention Agency
2005–06 Budget: Shelter Program Full Costs ❶
As of May 13, 2005

	Core	Expanded
Salaries	295,920	295,920
Payroll taxes	30,332	30,332
Training	3,600	3,600
Personnel expenses	329,852	329,852
Clients, direct assistance to	250,000	375,000
Conferences and meetings	1,000	1,000
Dues and subscriptions	1,000	1,000
Other professional fees	20,000	20,000
Printing and copying	1,000	1,000
Supplies	15,000	15,000
Travel	3,750	3,750
Non-personnel expenses	291,750	416,750
Total specific costs	621,602	746,602
% of FTEs	45.00%	45.00%
Allocation of common costs ❷	181,473	181,473
Expenses before overhead	803,075	928,075
% of direct costs	57.00%	57.00%
Allocation of admin costs ❸	108,200	108,200
Total expenses ❹	911,276	1,036,276
Shelter Nights		
Single women	2,190	2,190
Women with children	4,380	4,380
Infants/Toddlers	1,095	1,095
Children (2–12)	1,460	1,460
Teens (13–18)	730	730
Total Number of Nights	9,855	9,855
Cost per night ❺	$92.47	$105.15

❶ This report includes all of the budgeted expenses for the Shelter Program—including allocated common and administrative costs.

❷ The shelter program is allocated 45% of DV's common costs.

❸ The shelter program is allocated 57% of DV's administrative costs.

❹ This total is considerably more than the one presented in Figure 25, which only lists direct program costs.

❺ Notice how much the cost per night increases from Figure 25 once common and administrative costs are added.

Note that the cost per unit for core shelter services increases from $63.07/night (as shown in Figure 25) to $92.36/night (as shown in Figure 26) when DV includes allocations—an increase of 46 percent. Had DV not analyzed and applied such allocations, it would not be aware of the true costs of offering its service.

Estimating capital acquisitions

As described in Chapter 2, the acquisition of fixed assets (land, buildings, and equipment) is not considered an expense, and thus has not been included in the cost estimates so far. After talking with activity managers about their capital needs, the finance manager should develop a capital budget, which lists individual items to be purchased or improved and their estimated cost. Depending on the financing plan for these items, a forecast for the associated debt may also be necessary. Remember that these purchases require an outlay of cash, but are recorded as assets and depreciated over several years. Based on the existing fixed assets and planned acquisitions, the finance manager estimates the non-cash depreciation expense for the year. (See Figure 9 for an example of a depreciation schedule.)

During step two of the budgeting process, all activity managers are working simultaneously on estimating expenses. Ideally they are consulting with one another and the process is a standing agenda item at weekly or biweekly management team meetings. The finance manager is adding allocable common and administrative costs to each manager's initial estimates and building the capital budget. Once all activities have submitted a draft of expenses, it is time to plan for income.

3. Forecasting income

As with expenses, historical information, the experiences of others, and current considerations will form the basis for income estimates. Fees, contributions, and special events can often be accurately estimated by reviewing past experience and adjusting for current plans and economic climate. For small or new organizations—and for simple decisions in all kinds of organizations—making an educated guess may be the best forecasting method. More formal forecasting involves the application of statistical and mathematical techniques to historical data to make projections about the future. Both forecasting and predicting—from "seat of the pants" to highly complex modeling—are based on the premise that future events can be predicted based on patterns discovered through reviewing historical information. Although it may sound like an obvious point, beware that future events may not follow the patterns of the past.

Historical information, the experiences of others, and current considerations will form the basis for forecasting income.

Figure 27. 2005–06 Budget: Income Forecast

Domestic Violence Intervention & Prevention Agency
2005–06 Budget: Income Forecast
As of May 13, 2005

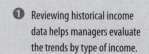

Funding Source	Actual 2002–03	Actual 2003–04	Forecast 2004–05	Budget 2005–06 Conservative	Optimistic
Annual campaign	29,565	19,385	15,000	15,000	35,000
Major gifts	19,750	22,500	18,000	20,000	30,000
Board donations	18,750	21,250	25,000	45,000	65,000
Endowment (individuals)	90,430	104,880	125,000	200,000	225,000
Events (net)	0	100,000	10,000	135,000	225,000
Foundation grants - unrestricted	22,500	12,750	115,000	125,000	175,000
Foundation grants - program restricted	439,000	439,000	550,000	835,000	925,000
Foundation grants - endowment				50,000	150,000
Government contracts	644,618	710,698	770,467	815,009	815,009
Interest/dividends	5,204	4,869	5,750	10,000	22,500
Investments	0	-8,246	0	0	0
Total income	1,269,817	1,427,086	1,634,217	2,250,009	2,667,509
Net assets released from restriction	387,541	570,746	453,000	450,000	550,000

❶ Reviewing historical income data helps managers evaluate the trends by type of income.

❷ At this time, staff are considering two income scenarios, conservative and optimistic.

In its assessment of income trends, DV uncovered several significant weaknesses in its fundraising performance to date. Study Figure 27, DV's Income Forecast, and note, in particular, the downward trend from 2001 to 2003 in certain fundraising categories: annual campaign and major gifts. The board and staff set aggressive goals related to income for the fiscal year, including an increase in both those categories, in endowment, and other areas. This forecast reflects the renewed energy of board members and an expectation that the fundraising environment has improved. As with expenses, at this juncture, DV is planning for two scenarios, labeled "conservative" and "optimistic" growth in the figure.

It is more difficult to forecast income when it comes in large chunks from few sources—such as foundations, corporations, and government agencies. When forecasting foundation and corporate grants and government contacts, it is essential to follow the accounting principle of matching revenue and expenses. For example, if a potential new source of funding will expand an existing program, you want to include (or exclude) both the new source of revenue and the associated new expenses in your budget. If you include only the new income, but exclude the associated new expenses, you've set yourself up for disaster.

If the organization typically receives restricted contributions, it will be necessary to budget for both unrestricted and restricted monies, especially in the situation of multiyear funding. In addition, organizations that routinely solicit and receive grants for specific projects need to include only the funds to be released from restriction in the budget period. For example, if DV receives a two-year grant for its support groups program in March 2003, the grant period would be April 2003 through March 2005. As DV's fiscal year is July 1 to June 30, this grant should be included in the budget over three of DV's fiscal years, as shown:

Year	Months	Percentage of Funds
02–03	3	12.5%
03–04	12	50.0%
04–05	9	37.5%
Total	24	100.0%

In addition, many organizations can benefit from adopting the more conservative approach of "discounting" the forecasted amount of the support based on the likelihood of receiving the grant. Note how in Figure 28, DV's Foundation Grant Detail, certain grant amounts are discounted from 25 percent to 75 percent depending on the perceived probability of receiving the grant—a wise practice.

With expenses and revenues estimated, it is time to strike a balance between the two.

4. Striking the balance

Once the initial estimates for income and expense have been made, the organization can see whether it has a balanced budget or whether income or expense exceeds the other. Remember, the budget does not have to balance at zero. An organization may choose to incur a deficit during a budget period. In so doing, it would be deciding to invest resources accumulated in prior years—perhaps to initiate or expand a program. On the other hand, the

Figure 28. 2005–06 Budget: Foundation Grant Detail

Domestic Violence Intervention & Prevention Agency
2005–06 Budget: Foundation Grant Detail
As of May 13, 2005

Committed Funds (100%)		Requested	Expected ❶	2005–06 ❷	2006–07
Allen Foundation	Support Groups	350,000	350,000	160,000	190,000
Belle Foundation	Support Groups	255,000	255,000	180,000	75,000
Community Foundation	Fundraising Planning	5,000	5,000	5,000	–
Detwiler Foundation	Endowment	10,000	10,000	10,000	–
Eastwood Fund	Endowment	10,000	10,000	10,000	–
Total committed funds		630,000	630,000	365,000	265,000
Discount	100%				
Highly Likely Funds (75%)					
Fong Family Fund	Support Groups	150,000	112,500	55,000	57,500
Greystone Foundation	Support Groups	150,000	112,500	50,000	62,500
Huntington Foundation	Endowment	10,000	7,500	7,500	–
Impact Fund	Endowment	10,000	7,500	7,500	–
Total highly likely funds		320,000	240,000	120,000	120,000
Discount	75%				
Likely Funds (50%)					
Jordon-Jackson Inc.	Endowment	30,000	15,000	15,000	–
Kirby and Kenny	Unrestricted	10,000	5,000	5,000	–
Landau Foundation	Unrestricted	45,000	22,500	22,500	–
Malcom X Fund	Unrestricted	25,000	12,500	12,500	–
Total likely funds		110,000	55,000	55,000	–
Discount	50%				
Possible Funds (25%)					
New Philanthrophy Fund	Unrestricted	200,000	50,000	50,000	–
One America Fund	Unrestricted	60,000	15,000	15,000	–
Progressive Partners	Unrestricted	30,000	7,500	7,500	–
Quackenbush Foundation	Unrestricted	50,000	12,500	12,500	–
Total possible funds		340,000	85,000	85,000	–
Discount	25%				
TOTAL		1,400,000	1,010,000	❸ 625,000	385,000

❶ A wise practice is to "discount" grant projections depending on the perceived probability of receiving the grant. The Expected column shows the discounted revenue amount from each funding source.

❷ Some expected funds will be available over two budget periods.

❸ DV plans for $625,000 in new grant income for 05–06.

organization may wish to budget for a surplus so as to build up the resources of the organization. Or it may decide to maintain the current level of resources and simply break even for the year. The leadership issue is that income and expense need to be in the relationship the organization *chooses*, rather than mechanically balanced.

While the relationship between income and expense in the budget is leadership's choice, remember our caution in Chapter 1 about the culture of scarcity that exists in many nonprofits. The only way for organizations to remain financially viable over the long term is to build an operating reserve. This can only be achieved by raising unrestricted contributions, by ensuring that fees for service exceed the cost for providing such services, or by some combination of contributions and fees in excess of costs. If a nonprofit organization breaks even or operates at a deficit year after year, it will eventually experience cash flow problems to an extent that expanding or sustaining services may become impossible.

In most cases, the first draft of the budget will include more expense than the organization can hope to fund. To strike the desired balance between income and expense, activities need to be re-evaluated and adjustments made. This is certainly the case at DV, where the initial draft, shown in Figure 29, First Budget Draft, matches the expanded program goals with DV's more conservative estimate of income. This draft projects a large operating deficit, which is inconsistent with board and staff financial goals.

Typically, the first draft may be in an unwieldy format. An alternative presentation, perhaps for the finance committee, would be Figure 30.

An organization that finds itself with a financially unfeasible first draft may consider increasing its fundraising goals. But, when reviewing the income budget, avoid the temptation of raising income estimates without changing the specific plans for generating the additional income. It is not enough just to say, "We'll try harder to raise money this year." An organization needs a carefully considered fundraising plan that is more *realistic* than *optimistic* when it comes to what it will cost to raise a dollar. If expenses need to be reduced, determine what each program activity would cost at different levels of intensity. For example, you might find that the cost of providing services for a program at one-half the current service level results in a decrease in costs by just one-third. The lesson here: Don't assume that benefits and costs move together—with each additional dollar spent resulting in an additional dollar of benefit. "Economics of scale" are present in most projects, and beyond a certain point, additional expenses may bring a diminished return. As a result, there may be some programs where a large reduction in expenses will result in less reduction in services than in other programs.

GOALS

Remember, the budget does not have to balance at zero. An organization may choose to incur a deficit or budget for a surplus.

Figure 29. 2005–06 Budget: First Draft – Expanded Program & Conservative Income

Domestic Violence Intervention & Prevention Agency
2005–06 Budget: First Draft – Expanded Program & Conservative Income
As of May 29, 2005

	Program Activities		Supporting Activities				
	Shelter Services	Support Groups	Admin- istration	Fund- raising	Common Costs	Total 2005–06	Total 2004–05
Contributions	–	–	–	80,000	–	80,000	58,000
Fundraising events - net	–	–	–	135,000	–	135,000	125,000
Foundation grants	–	–	–	125,000	–	125,000	115,000
Total support	–	–	–	340,000	–	340,000	298,000
Government contracts	815,009	–	–	–	–	815,009	770,467
Interest and dividends	–	–	10,000	–	–	10,000	5,750
Unrealized gain (loss) on investments	–	–	–	–	–	–	–
Total revenue	815,009	–	10,000	–	–	825,009	776,217
Net assets released from restriction	–	445,000	–	5,000	–	450,000	453,000
Total income	815,009	445,000	10,000	345,000	–	1,615,009	1,527,217
Salaries	295,920	194,450	106,000	115,500	88,960	800,830	804,660
Payroll taxes	30,332	19,931	10,865	11,839	9,118	82,085	82,478
Employee benefits	–	–	–	–	80,083	80,083	80,466
Training	3,600	500	500	–	1,000	5,600	5,600
Personnel expenses	329,852	214,881	117,365	127,339	179,161	968,598	973,204
Accounting	–	–	17,500	–	–	17,500	15,000
Bank charges	–	–	5,000	–	–	5,000	3,500
Building expenses	–	–	–	–	27,500	27,500	25,000
Clients, direct assistance to	375,000	–	–	–	–	375,000	150,000
Conferences and meetings	1,000	10,000	2,500	2,000	2,000	17,500	17,500
Depreciation	–	–	–	–	38,897	38,897	54,000
Dues and subscriptions	1,000	2,300	100	250	–	3,650	3,650
Equipment rental/maintenance	–	–	–	–	3,200	3,200	3,200
Insurance	–	–	–	–	29,000	29,000	23,000
Interest	–	–	–	–	8,016	8,016	8,007
Other professional fees	20,000	87,000	2,500	25,000	5,000	139,500	35,500
Postage and delivery	–	–	–	4,000	8,000	12,000	12,000
Printing and copying	1,000	5,000	–	10,000	–	16,000	16,000
Supplies	15,000	10,000	–	2,500	24,000	51,500	49,100
Telephone	–	–	–	–	36,000	36,000	31,800
Travel	3,750	15,000	500	1,000	–	20,250	20,250
Utilities	–	–	–	–	42,500	42,500	38,000
Non-personnel expenses	416,750	129,300	28,100	44,750	224,113	843,013	505,507
Total specific costs	746,602	344,181	145,465	172,089	403,274	1,811,611	1,478,711
Change in net assets	68,407	100,819	(135,465)	172,911	(403,274)	(196,602)	48,507

Figure 30. 2005–06 Budget: First Draft – Summarized

Domestic Violence Intervention & Prevention Agency
2005–06 Budget: First Draft – Summarized
As of May 29, 2005

	Program Activities		Supporting Activities				
	Shelter Services	Support Groups	Admin-istration	Fund-raising	Common Costs	Total 2005–06	Total 2004–05
Contributions	–	–	–	80,000	–	80,000	58,000
Fundraising events - net	–	–	–	135,000	–	135,000	125,000
Foundation grants	–	–	–	125,000	–	125,000	115,000
Total support	–	–	–	340,000	–	340,000	298,000
Government contracts	815,009	–	–	–	–	815,009	770,467
Interest and dividends	–	–	10,000	–	–	10,000	5,750
Unrealized gain (loss) on investments	–	–	–	–	–	–	–
Total revenue	815,009	–	10,000	–	–	825,009	776,217
							–
Net assets released from restriction	–	445,000	–	5,000	–	450,000	453,000
Total income	815,009	445,000	10,000	345,000	–	1,615,009	1,527,217
Personnel expenses ❶	329,852	214,881	117,365	127,339	179,161	968,598	973,204
Non-personnel expenses	416,750	129,300	28,100	44,750	224,113	843,013	505,507
Total specific costs	746,602	344,181	145,465	172,089	403,274	1,811,611	1,478,711
% of FTEs	45.00%	31.00%	11.00%	13.00%	-100.00%	0.00%	–
Allocation of common costs	181,473	125,015	44,360	52,426	(403,274)	–	–
Expenses before overhead	928,075	469,196	189,825	224,514	–	1,811,611	1,478,711
Change before overhead	(113,066)	(24,196)	(179,825)	120,486	–	(196,602)	48,507
% of direct costs	57.00%	29.00%	-100.00%	14.00%	0.00%	(0)	–
Allocation of admin costs	108,200	55,049	(189,825)	26,576	–	(0)	–
Total expenses	1,036,276	524,245	–	251,090	–	1,811,611	1,478,710
							❷
Change in net assets	(221,267)	(79,245)	10,000	93,910	–	(196,602)	48,507

❶ The summarized budget first draft does not itemize personnel and non-personnel expenses.

❷ A large operating deficit does not meet DV's financial goals. Activity costs may have to be reconsidered.

When reviewing the income budget, avoid the temptation of raising income estimates without changing the specific plans for generating the additional income. It is not enough just to say, "We'll try harder to raise money this year."

Two additional practices help the organization strike a balance in the budget:

1. Contingency planning
2. Cash flow projection

In striking the balance between goals and available resources, DV's management team and board face competing demands. They are committed to dedicating more resources to direct client financial assistance, but shifting resources to client assistance translates into fewer resources for other organizational activities, such as administration and development. They are also committed to addressing some of the financial weaknesses they identified in Chapter 3. Furthermore, they are uncertain as to whether they can meet their optimistic income forecast. These uncertainties and tensions are normal factors in most every annual planning process. In these cases, wise organizations prepare contingencies.

Contingency planning

In an environment of uncertain income or expense, a contingency budget can be a useful tool. In this approach, the activity managers calculate the costs of operating at different levels and develop two or more budgets that reflect different scenarios. Typically, the first budget operates on the assumption that activities will be cut back or maintained to provide the minimum level of service to which the organization is irrevocably committed; this becomes the base cost. The second budget assumes additional resources with corresponding additional costs. Often, this second budget reflects an assumption of economies of scale: an increase in the level of activity results in a decrease in the total cost per mission unit. Estimating expenses for programs at different levels can reveal the level at which maximum economies of scale occur.

Given the undesirable deficit in the first draft of its budget, DV is using contingency budgeting to plan for two different levels of income and expense—one fairly certain and one more optimistic. In Figure 31, DV's Contingency Budget, DV shows the various assumptions in its contingency budget with the following labels:

- Realistic Income: Funds that are either already committed or represent conservative estimates.
- Optimistic Income: Estimates for additional fundraising income that is likely but not certain.
- Fundraising Goal: The combination of the realistic and optimistic income estimates.
- Core Expenses: Essential expenses with no expansion of services.
- Incremental Expenses: Additional expenses if new funds are secured.
- Total Expenses: Combination of core expenses and incremental expenses.

Figure 31. 2005–06 Budget: Contingency Plan – Unrestricted

Domestic Violence Intervention & Prevention Agency
2005–06 Budget: Contingency Plan – Unrestricted
As of June 3, 2005

	Realistic Income & Core Expenses	Optimistic Income & Incremental Expenses	Fundraising Goals & Total Expenses	Notes
Contributions	80,000	50,000	130,000	Additional new direct mail campaign
Fundraising events - net	135,000	90,000	225,000	Includes new event
Foundation grants	125,000	50,000	175,000	General operating support
Total support	340,000	190,000	530,000	
Government contracts	815,009	–	815,009	
Interest and dividends	10,000	12,500	22,500	
Unrealized gain (loss) on investments	–		–	
Total revenue	825,009	12,500	837,509	
Net assets released from restriction	450,000	100,000	550,000	Chinese support groups
Total income	1,615,009	302,500	1,917,509	
Shelter Services	803,075	125,000	928,075	Direct assistance
Support Groups	394,196	75,000	469,196	Chinese support groups
Administration	189,825	–	189,825	
Fundraising	199,514	25,000	224,514	Endowment campaign consultant
Total expenses	1,586,611	225,000	1,811,611	
Change in net assets	28,398	77,500	105,898	
Beginning net assets	168,690	–	168,690	
Ending net assets	197,088	77,500	274,588	
Liquid operating reserve	149,340		226,841	
Monthly expenses	132,218		150,968	
Liquid operating reserve in months	1.13		1.50	
Overhead ratio:	25%		23%	
Fundraising ratio (unrestricted)	1.70		2.36	

❶ The contingency budget shows two different scenarios that forecast different levels of income and expenses.

❷ The optimistic column adds more income (and expenses).

❸ The Notes column describes how the new resources and costs are factored.

❹ These indicators ensure that the budget is responding to the assessment and goal-setting process.

The "Notes" column of the contingency budget presentation alerts the reader to what additional resources and costs are factored. Notice that in its optimistic funding scenario, DV will add Chinese language support groups, increase financial assistance to clients, and employ a consultant to maximize endowment growth.

Cash flow projection

At this juncture—when staff are close to a final draft for consideration by the board—the finance manager should also develop an accompanying cash flow projection. This is important because budgets are accrual-based (matching revenue and expenses) and as a result, cash shortages can go unanticipated. For example, even if an organization has a balanced budget for the year (for example, it plans to raise and spend $1 million), it may not receive the majority of budgeted income until late in the budget period—while its expenses may be spread evenly throughout the period. A cash flow projection will help foresee cash flow problems and plan for solutions. As Figure 32 shows, DV's first quarter will be tricky. As a result, DV is planning to use its new line of credit. You can see that DV will need to borrow $75,000 from its line of credit to cover the cash shortage during the first quarter (and have at least a half month's cash on hand for emergencies), and it will pay it back during the second quarter. This format also shows the projected balance in DV's investment account—which will help the board finance/investment committee and finance staff plan for maximum return.

5. Approving the Plan

While the staff is responsible for developing the budget, the board—acting in its governance role—thoroughly reviews and approves the budget. The best budget presentations clearly link the organization's goals to the financial forecasts. In DV's case, the goals are presented before the financial projections. Figure 33, DV's Budget Goals, shows DV's goals, objectives, the means of measuring progress, and a comparison of the forecasted budget with the current year's budget. One of the key aspects of this presentation to the board is the inclusion of measurements—or how DV will know if it is making the desired progress. In presenting measurements, DV's staff set up a means of holding themselves accountable to the board (and themselves) for meeting the goals they've set. Without measurements, performance is difficult to track and too easy to explain away when it is not optimal.

Figure 34, Final Budget Presentation, is the budget presented to the board. Note that the budget is "rolled up"—with expenses presented by functional classification—allowing the board to exercise its oversight duties without getting mired in budget minutiae. Also, notice that DV management decided to

While the staff is responsible for developing the budget, the board—acting in its governance role—thoroughly reviews and approves the budget.

Figure 32. 2005–06 Budget: Cash Flow Projection

Domestic Violence Intervention & Prevention Agency
2005–05 Budget: Cash Flow Projection
As of June 3, 2005

	Total Budget	1st Quarter 7/1–9/30/05	2nd Quarter 10/1–12/31/05	3rd Quarter 1/1–3/31/06	4th Quarter 4/1–6/30/06	
Opening Cash Balance	175,000	175,000	49,125	121,100	148,896	❶ DV plans to draw $125,000 on its line of credit in order to cover the cash shortage in the first quarter.
Fundraising	415,000	100,000	215,000	50,000	50,000	
Foundation grants	1,010,000	25,000	300,000	350,000	335,000	
Government contracts	815,009	125,009	530,000	75,000	85,000	
Interest and dividends	10,000	2,500	2,500	2,500	2,500	
Total Inflows	2,250,009	252,509	1,047,500	477,500	472,500	
Personnel	968,598	242,148	242,150	242,150	242,150	
Operating	843,013	228,946	205,875	205,054	203,138	
Capital	29,790	29,790	–	–	–	
Total Outflows	1,841,401	500,884	448,025	447,204	445,288	
Cash Available	583,608	❶ (73,375)	648,600	151,396	176,108	
From (To) Line of Credit	0	125,000	(125,000)	–	–	
From (To) Investments	(410,000)	(2,500)	(402,500)	(2,500)	(2,500)	
Closing Cash Balance	173,608	49,125	121,100	48,896	173,608	
Beginning Investments	105,000	105,000	107,500	510,000	512,500	
Ending Investments	515,000	107,500	510,000	512,500	515,000	

propose the core services budget—the more conservative of the two scenarios they explored during their planning process—for approval by the board. The board's finance committee should meet with key staff to review the proposed budget and ask specific questions about the assumptions underneath it. Once satisfied, the committee chair should present the goals and corresponding budget to a full board meeting and recommend the budget's approval.

Revising the budget

There is considerable debate about whether organizations should revise their budgets once they have been approved by their boards to reflect new information and projections. The motivations to revise a budget vary, from the desire to have a better monitoring tool (comparing actuals to invalid projections can be frustrating), to an executive's desire to keep from looking bad in front of

Figure 33. 2005–06 Budget: Goals and Objectives – with Measurements

Domestic Violence Intervention & Prevention Agency
2005–06 Budget: Goals and Objectives (with measurements)
As of June 17, 2005

Overall Goal	2005–06 Objective	Measurement ❶	2005–06 ❷	2004–05
Stabilize programs and ensure highest quality	Salary increases to all staff	Salary increase	8%	0%
	Replace computers and equipment	Capital purchases	29,790	1,057
	Increase direct client support	Budget for direct assistance	250,000	150,000
Improve on key financial health indicators	Build liquid operating reserve	Months of reserve	1.02	0.72
	Reduce overhead rate	Overhead ratio	25%	29%
	Obtain line of credit	Available credit	75,000	0
Maximize fund-raising effective-ness	Increase endowment income	Permanently restricted net assets	355,000	105,000
	Increase board role in fundraising	Fundraising return (unrestrict-ed)	1.69	1.27
		Fundraising return (total)	7.09	3.85
	Build temporarily restricted balance	Ending net assets	756,004	371,004
	Maximize cost recovery in foundation grants	Support groups' performance	(4,114)	(28,140)

❶ It is important to include measurements with goals—this allows DV to track progress and be accountable for meeting the goals they set.

❷ Specific numerical measurements are set and a comparison to last year is provided for context.

his or her board. The downside of eliminating an inaccurate budget is that the organization loses the opportunity to reflect on what went wrong with its planning process. We recommend that organizations do both a three- and six-month review of how the budget is holding up to actual financial activity. If there are substantial differences between the plan and the reality, staff may develop and bring a revised budget to the finance committee for approval. The financial leader may also ask the finance manger to add a projections column to the budget-to-actual reports. This strategy both preserves the original story and provides readers with a more up-to-date prediction of where the organization is going to land.

Figure 34. 2005–06 Budget: Final Presentation for Board Approval

Domestic Violence Intervention & Prevention Agency
2005–06 Budget: Final Presentation for Board Approval
As of June 17, 2005

❶	Unrestricted	Temporarily Restricted	Permanently Restricted	Total
Contributions	80,000	–	200,000	280,000
Fundraising events - net	135,000	–	–	135,000
Foundation grants	125,000	835,000	50,000	1,010,000
Total support	340,000	835,000	250,000	1,425,000
Government contracts	815,009	–	–	815,009
Interest and dividends	10,000	–	–	10,000
Unrealized gain (loss) on investments	–	–	–	–
Total revenue	825,009	–	–	825,009
Net assets released from restriction	450,000	(450,000)		–
Total income	1,615,009	385,000	250,000	2,250,009
Shelter Services	801,731	–	–	801,731
Support Groups	394,196	–	–	394,196
Administration	189,825	–	–	189,825
Fundraising	200,859	–	–	200,859
Total expenses	1,586,611	–	–	1,586,611
Change in net assets	28,398	385,000	250,000	663,398
Beginning net assets	300,000	371,004	105,000	776,004
Ending net assets	328,398	756,004	355,000	1,439,402
Liquid operating reserve	149,340			
Monthly expenses	132,218			
Liquid operating reserve in months	1.13			
Efficiency Ratios:				
Overhead ratio	25%			
Fundraising ratio (unrestricted)	1.70			
Fundraising ratio (total)	7.14			

❶ In the final budget report for the boards, the budget is "rolled up," allowing the board to exercise oversight without getting mired in budget minutiae.

❷ Note that the board presentation of the budget shows expenses functionally, not line-by-line.

❸ This version includes plans for all temporarily and permanently restricted funds.

Evaluate Your Financial Planning

Take the organizational evaluation in Figure 35 to consider the current quality of financial planning at your organization. Elena's answers and comments are highlighted for your reference under "comments." A complete blank version of the evaluation tool can be found in Appendix B.

Summary

In years when the organization is not undergoing a strategic planning process, the budgeting process is typically the only formal vehicle for strategic thinking and planning. The financial leader includes all voices in the process: program, development, finance, and governance (board). When it is responsive to a thorough assessment of strengths, weaknesses, opportunities, and threats, the budget becomes a true reflection of the organizational goals and work plan. Once approved, a good budget becomes an instigator of discussions and a means for helping everyone own the financial progress of the organization.

The budget is a critical tool. But as a financial leader, you also need to be able to *communicate* to staff, board, and a host of others—from financial experts to total beginners—about the financial progress of the organization. In Chapter 5, you will learn how to do this.

Figure 35.   Financial Planning Assessment

Category	Red	Yellow	Green	Comments	Action Plan
Budget Process	We have no annual budget	The annual budget is not a true reflection of our work plan for the year.	The annual budget is our planning and monitoring tool.	None	N/A
Participation	The finance manager and/or executive director creates the budget.	The finance manager and/or executive director creates the budget with some input from other managers.	The budgeting process is inclusive and demands that all activity managers engage in meaningful planning for the year to come.	Some of the management staff are still learning how to forecast income and expenses, so I tend to help them.	Work towards a model where each member of the team has the skills and interest to create and manage his/her own budget.
Expense Forecasting	We estimate costs based solely on our known grants and contracts.	We estimate our costs based on both what's known in our grants and contracts and what it would cost to do the best work possible.	We start by estimating what it would cost to do the best work possible, regardless of who funds it.	Given our reliance on government contracts for the shelter, it's pretty hard to build our budget from scratch.	Work toward a true activity-centered budgeting model.
Income Projection	We do no historical analysis and regularly overestimate income for the year.	Based on historical analysis, we generally come close to accurately forecasting income.	Using historical analysis and current data gathering, we forecast income realistically.	Although we try very hard, we find it quite difficult to accurately predict foundation grants.	Develop new analysis tools.
Striking the Balance	Leadership thinks a good budget is a balanced budget.	Leadership strives for a balanced or slight surplus budget.	Leadership considers available resources and current opportunities in deciding whether to build a deficit, balanced, or surplus budget.	None	N/A
Revision	We "true up" our budget throughout the year to correct for inaccurate planning.	At midyear we consider revising our budget if there are material inaccuracies in the expenses and/or income targets.	While we sometimes have to revise the budget, we use contingency budgeting to prepare board and staff for likely scenarios.	None	N/A

5. Communicating Progress

The final element of financial leadership is communicating progress toward the established goals with the organization's key stakeholders. Communicating about finance is a high art; it requires engaging people who are untrained in finance in meaningful financial discussions, sharing financial information that may at times be uncomfortable or unflattering, and demonstrating financial accountability to the people and institutions that use, fund, and regulate your work as a nonprofit business. But the most important outcome of ongoing, clear communication is the ability of an executive director, the board, and staff to anticipate financial challenges, revise plans, and avoid uninformed decisions that could lead the organization into financial crisis.

Financial reports are the primary tool for communicating financial progress. Some financial reports come right out of an accounting system, while others—such as an annual report to the community and IRS Form 990—use figures from the accounting system but are created outside of it. As the financial leader, you will likely not be responsible for creating any of these reports, but you are responsible for ensuring that each of these audiences gets the financial information it needs. Moreover, it is in your best interests that these audiences get financial information because you seek their partnership in monitoring progress and continually evaluating organizational goals and objectives.

Depending upon how you are staffing the financial function at your nonprofit organization, you will be working with a staff finance manager, an independent bookkeeper, or a CPA to develop your financial reports. In any case, it's important to remember your leadership role. In our work with community-based nonprofits, we often encounter executive directors, program managers, and boards of directors who are very unhappy with the financial reporting they receive but who feel unable to change it. Although you may know nothing about the accounting software being used or about bookkeeping per se, it is your role and responsibility to work with your producer of financial reports to get the information that your key audiences need—in the format they need it in. This can take time and negotiation, but it is critical. If in the end the person you are working with is unable or unwilling to make the changes and improvements to the reporting that you seek, it is probably time to look for someone new who can carry out these functions.

Match the Message to the Audience

There are five audiences that a financial leader should keep informed and communicate with about the organization's financial progress:

- Staff (all staff and the management team)
- Board (full board and finance committee)
- Funders (governmental and nongovernmental)
- Constituents (clients or beneficiaries, donors, community partners, and other external stakeholders)
- IRS/Regulators

These five audiences vary in what financial information they need or require and the frequency with which they need or require it. They also vary in terms of the financial story you, as the leader, want them to read and understand. For instance, a program manager who is running a single program at your organization needs to read and understand a different financial story than your board treasurer does. The IRS mandates a detailed annual financial report, while clients and community supporters want to read a more basic overview of your financial progress each year.

Let's look at the types of information that you, as a leader, want various audiences to have, as well as what actions you want them to take based upon it. We'll continue to use the Domestic Violence Intervention & Prevention Agency as an example throughout. Except for the Annual Report and Form 990, all reports in this chapter are midyear reports—that is, they reflect financial activity for the six-month period ending on December 31, 2005.

Program managers

Staff who are responsible for a limited portion of the budget should get reports that reflect their responsibilities. For instance, Sherri, the shelter program manager at DV, is responsible for developing the shelter's expense budget and managing expenses within that budget. A good monthly report for her would look like Figure 36, DV's Shelter Program Expense Report.

Figure 36. Shelter Program Expense Report

Domestic Violence Intervention & Prevention Agency
Shelter Program Expense Report
For the Six Months Ending December 31, 2005

	Budget	This Month	YTD	Remaining ❶ $	%
Salaries	295,920	24,002	133,164	162,756	55%
Payroll taxes	30,332	2,495	15,773	14,559	48%
Training	3,600	0	1,980	1,620	45%
Personnel expenses	329,852	26,497	150,917	178,935	54%
Clients, direct assistance to	250,000	54,584	119,542	130,458	52%
Conferences and meetings	1,000	125	741	259	26%
Dues and subscriptions	1,000	217	684	316	32%
Other professional fees	20,000	2,575	4,852	15,148	76%
Printing and copying	1,000	73	874	126	13%
Supplies	15,000	2,394	4,587	10,413	69%
Travel	3,750	140	1,258	2,492	66%
Non-personnel expenses	291,750	60,108	132,538	159,212	55%
Total expenses before allocations	621,602	86,605	283,455	338,147	❷ 54%
Shelter nights					
Single women	2,190	215	1,484	706	32%
Women with children	4,380	458	1,964	2,416	55%
Infants/toddlers	1,095	125	458	637	58%
Children (2–12)	1,460	158	1,078	382	26%
Teens (13–18)	730	98	589	141	19%
Total number of nights	9,855	1,054	5,573	4,282	❸ 43%

❶ This report shows shelter expenses for the first half of the fiscal year. Thus, it is expected that 50% of the income remains to be raised and 50% of the expenses are yet unspent.

❷ The Shelter Program is doing better than planned on expenses. Midway through the year, they have 54% of expenses remaining.

❸ The Shelter Program is ahead of schedule in terms of units of service provided. Midway through the year, they have only 43% of their budgeted units left to fulfill.

As the program manager, Sherri's responsibilities are managing expenses within the budget and meeting goals for shelter nights provided across DV's key service populations. She is not responsible for approving common costs such as rent and telephone or agency administrative costs, so those are not included in this report. The financial leader, Elena, wants Sherri to manage this budget and control expenses if things are getting off track. As you can see by looking at the "% Remaining" column on the far right of the table, Sherri is on track and there is no action warranted at this time.

Development director

The development director is another staff person responsible for a specific portion of an agency's work. For example, Dana, DV's development director, must track the various income streams compared to budget as well as the expenses of her department. Dana's report is Figure 37, Development Department Report.

Again, looking at the "% Remaining" column, this report alerts DV—and Dana—that in fact certain income streams are not performing according to plans. Half way into the year, unrestricted fundraising—the annual campaign,

Figure 37. Development Department Report

Domestic Violence Intervention & Prevention Agency
Development Department Report
For the Six Months Ended December 31, 2005

Funding Source	Budget 2005–06	Actual 12/31/2005	Remaining $	%
Annual campaign	15,000	6,852	8,148	54%
Major gifts	20,000	8,751	11,249	56%
Board donations	45,000	15,874	29,126	65%
Events (net)	135,000	62,415	72,585	54%
Foundation grants - unrestricted	125,000	45,000	80,000	64%
Total unrestricted support	340,000	138,892	201,108	59%
Endowment (individuals)	200,000	194,500	5,500	3%
Foundation grants - program restricted	835,000	955,000	(120,000)	-14%
Foundation grants - endowment	50,000	70,000	(20,000)	-40%
Total restricted support	1,085,000	1,219,500	(134,500)	-12%
Total support	1,425,000	1,358,392	66,608	5%
Government contracts	815,009	460,887	354,122	43%
Interest/dividends	10,000	8,754	1,246	12%
Investments	–	2,251	(2,251)	n/a
Total revenue	825,009	471,892	353,117	43%
Total income	2,250,009	1,830,284	419,725	19%
Fundraising expenses	199,514	135,214	64,300	32%
Fundraising effectiveness: ❸				
Unrestricted support	1.70	1.03		
Total support	7.14	10.05		
Total income	11.28	13.54		

❶ These percentages alert DV that unrestricted income streams are not performing as expected. The development director should create revised projections for each of these income categories.

❷ On the other hand, DV is far ahead of schedule in raising restricted contributions.

❸ Fundraising return is a key indicator that DV elected to monitor in 2005–06. While their effectiveness for total income is better than planned, the return on unrestricted support is worse than planned.

board donations, and foundation grants—is falling short. At the same time, contributions to the endowment as well as restricted contributions from foundations are ahead of pace. In other words, DV is meeting (and exceeding) some of the income goals it set for itself for 2005–06 and not meeting others. It is likely that some of its contributors responded to special requests for the endowment fund and therefore have not made their normal annual gifts. Moreover, staff time focused on the growth of the endowment may have limited DV's attention to cultivating annual campaign donations.

The action warranted here is a revised projection from Dana on where the agency is now likely to end the year in each of these income categories. As we talked about in the discussion of monitoring budget variance in Chapter 3, spending according to budget is meaningless if you are not also generating income according to budget. It's the relationship between the two that is the target. Thus leaders have to call for new projections when they have any evidence that the agreed upon plan is unlikely to come to fruition. With a revised projection of income, DV will then have to contain expenses and/or accept a different financial outcome for the year.

Management team and board finance committee

The management team and finance committee of a board of directors are responsible for tracking the financial condition of activities and the organization overall, so they need a complete set of financial statements each month or quarter. Here is the complete monitoring package for DV's financial leaders:

1. Statement of Financial Position (page 26)

2. Statement of Activities (page 25)

3. Budgeted Statement of Activities – Unrestricted (page 42)

4. Functional Income and Expenses (page 46)

5. Restricted Funds Detail (page 57)

6. Updated Cash Flow (page 99)

We have seen a number of these key reports in previous chapters. In this discussion of communication, let's focus on the Budgeted Statement of Activities, as presented in Figure 38, page 98.

At this point midyear, DV's management team has some decisions to make based on their monitoring of actual income and expense to budget. Just as Dana, the development manager, is revising her projections for income, department heads will have to consider revised expenses as well. Elena (the executive director) will also work with DV's board treasurer to develop a presentation to the full board alerting them to the situation and preparing them for revised projections and outcomes for the year. Certainly, Elena will press board

---

Six Financial Statements for Leaders

1. Statement of Financial Position

2. Statement of Activities

3. Budgeted Statement of Activities – Unrestricted

4. Functional Income and Expenses

5. Restricted Funds Detail

6. Updated Cash Flow

Figure 38. Budgeted Statement of Activities – Unrestricted

Domestic Violence Intervention & Prevention Agency
Budgeted Statement of Activity – Unrestricted
For the Six Months Ending December 31, 2005

	YTD Actual	YTD Budget	Variance B/(W)	Annual Budget	$ Remaining	% Remaining
Contributions	31,477 ❶	40,000	(8,523)	80,000	48,523	61%
Fundraising events - net	62,415	67,500	(5,085)	135,000	72,585	54%
Foundation grants	45,000	62,500	(17,500)	125,000	80,000	64%
Total support	138,892	170,000	(31,108)	340,000	201,108	59%
Government contracts	460,887	407,505	53,382	815,009	354,122	43%
Interest and dividends	8,754	5,000	3,754	10,000	1,246	12%
Unrealized gain (loss) on investments	2,251	–	2,251	–	(2,251)	n/a
Total revenue	471,892	412,505	59,387	825,009	353,117	43%
Net assets released from restriction	220,020	225,000	(4,980)	450,000	229,980	51%
Total income	830,804	807,505 ❷	23,299	1,615,009	784,205	49%
Shelter Services	398,547	401,538	2,991	803,075	404,528	50%
Support Groups	194,012	197,098	3,086	394,196	200,184	51%
Administration	98,754	94,913	(3,841)	189,825	91,071	48%
Fundraising	135,214	99,757	(35,457)	199,514	64,300	32%
Total expenses	826,527	793,306 ❷	(33,221)	1,586,610	760,083	48%
Change in net assets	4,277	14,199	(9,922)	28,399	24,122	85%
Beginning net assets	298,547	300,000	(1,453)	168,690		
Ending net assets	302,824	314,199	(11,375)	197,089	24,122	12%

Liquid operating reserve	123,767
Monthly expenses	137,755
Liquid operating reserve in months	0.90
Overhead ratio	28%

❶ DV's executive director will press the board to fulfill their own giving commitments, since this line-item is underperforming.

❷ Given the fairly significant variance between planned and actual income and expenses, an updated projection will be created (see Figure 39).

members to fulfill their own giving commitments as soon as possible, since the board giving line item is one of the under-producers. Given the material variance between planned and actual income, Elena has instructed the finance manager to prepare an updated projection for the rest of the year. Figure 39, Updated Projection, shows DV's revised projection for 2005–06.

Figure 39. Updated Projection

Domestic Violence Intervention & Prevention Agency
Updated Projection - Unrestricted
As of January 20, 2006

	Annual Budget	1st Qtr Actual	2nd Qtr Actual	YTD Actual	3rd Qtr Projected	4th Qtr Projected	Revised Projection	Variance B/(W)
Contributions	80,000	12,540	18,937	31,477	25,741	22,584	79,802	(198)
Fundraising events - net	135,000	21,540	40,875	62,415	–	65,000	127,415	(7,585)
Foundation grants	125,000	15,000	30,000	45,000	32,500	45,000	122,500	(2,500)
Total support	340,000	49,080	89,812	138,892	58,241	132,584	329,717	(10,283)
Government contracts	815,009	204,580	256,307	460,887	180,000	174,122	815,009	–
Interest and dividends	10,000	5,147	3,607	8,754	8,500	8,500	25,754	15,754
Unrealized gain (loss) on investments	–		2,251	2,251	2,500	2,500	7,251	7,251
Total revenue	825,009	209,727	262,165	471,892	191,000	185,122	848,014	23,005
Net assets released from restriction	450,000	95,478	124,542	220,020	125,000	125,000	470,020	20,020
Total income	1,615,009	354,285	476,519	830,804	374,241	442,706	1,647,751 ❶	32,742
Shelter Services	801,731	201,602	196,945	398,547	201,501	200,154	800,202	1,529
Support Groups	394,196	102,547	91,465	194,012	98,541	102,584	395,137	(941)
Administration	189,825	55,140	43,614	98,754	48,521	49,587	196,862	(7,037)
Fundraising	200,859	51,478	83,736	135,214	52,410	48,521	236,145	(35,286)
Total expenses	1,586,611	410,767	415,760	826,527	400,973	400,846	1,628,346 ❷	(41,735)
Change in net assets	28,398	(56,482)	60,759	4,277	(26,732)	41,860	19,405	(8,993)
Beginning net assets	300,000	298,547	242,065	298,547	302,824	276,092	298,547	(1,453)
Ending net assets	328,398	242,065	302,824	302,824	276,092	317,952	317,952	❸ (10,446)

❶ The development manager updated income projections, increasing income by $32,742.

❷ The finance manager also increased projected spending.

❸ With these new projections, DV predicts they'll end the year with $10,446 less in net assets than it originally budgeted.

Full staff and board

For the full staff and board we suggest using a "scorecard" and narrative based on the specific goals set by the organization for the year (and described in Chapter 4). Provided quarterly at staff and board meetings, the kind of presentation in Figure 40, Performance Scorecard, is far more likely to elicit questions and comments than a traditional stack of financial statements, which hardly any staff and board know how to read. Make financial progress an agenda item at your staff meetings once per quarter so that staff become accustomed to monitoring financial progress. Encourage people to ask questions and make comments. If the organization gets off track financially and has to make hard decisions, such as closing a program or laying off staff, the financial leader will have far more credibility and perhaps even empathy from staff if they have been kept informed along the way.

As you can see, DV's scorecard at six months captures graphically its success and challenges thus far in 2005–06. Using the red, yellow, green format and focusing upon organizationally specific goals fosters high-level discussion of implications and strategy. It allows staff and board who might otherwise be intimidated by the "business" part of a meeting's agenda to access the most important indicators of financial progress.

Most of the key measurements included on the scorecard are calculated using information from DV's Statement of Activities (see Figure 41, page 102).

Figure 40. Performance Scorecard

Domestic Violence Intervention & Prevention Agency
Performance Scorecard
For the Six Months Ending December 31, 2005

Overall Goal	2005–06 Objective	Measurement	Full Year Budget	Actual 12/31/05	Variance B/(W)	Status
Stabilize programs and ensure highest quality	• Salary increases to all staff	• Salary increase	8%	8%	-	Green
	• Replace computers and equipment	• Capital purchases	29,790	29,790	-	Green
	• Increase direct client support	• Budget (actual) for direct assistance	250,000	119,542	(130,458)	Yellow
Improve on key financial health indicators	• Build cash reserve	• Months of reserve	1.02	0.83	(0.19)	Red
	• Reduce overhead rate	• Overhead ratio	24.62%	28.31%	-3.68%	Yellow
	• Obtain line of credit	• Available credit	75,000	200,000	125,000	Green
Maximize fund-raising effectiveness	• Increase endowment income	• Permanently restricted net assets	355,000	369,500	14,500	Green
	• Increase board role in fundraising	• Fundraising return (unrestricted)	1.69	1.03	(0.67)	Yellow
		• Fundraising return (total)	7.09	10.05	2.95	Green
	• Build temporarily restricted balance	• Ending net assets	756,004	1,105,984	349,980	Green
	• Maximize cost recovery in foundation grants	• Support groups performance	(4,114)	(419)	3,695	Green

HIGHLIGHTS	Salary increases:	The full 8% increase was funded—our first salary increase in three years!
	Capital purchases:	All of the planned equipment purchases were completed on schedule, and staff are currently being trained on using the new client database program.
	Endowment fundraising:	We have completed the campaign, raising $14,500 over our goals!
	Line of credit:	As planned, we secured a $200,000 line of credit with our bank.
	Cost recovery:	We have secured foundation grants to cover (almost) all of the support group costs for this year, AND we have commitments for all of next year's costs!!!
MIXED RESULTS	Direct client support:	We are a little behind our goal in distributing client support dollars (although we did secure a grant to help pay these costs). We are investigating the situation and will report back next month.
	Overhead costs:	Due to higher than expected fundraising costs (associated with the endowment campaign), our overhead ratio is higher than we like.
	Fundraising Return:	Our higher costs in fundraising have reduced our unrestricted return ratio. The 'total' ratio is on track.
LOW LIGHTS	Cash Reserve:	Given our focus on the endowment campaign and renegotiating with our funders to cover the costs of support groups, we have dropped the ball a bit on our unrestricted fundraising. In hindsight, it was probably not realistic to take on *all* of these challenges at once. Although we are showing a small surplus at this three-quarter mark, we are barely keeping pace with inflation. We *must* focus our attention toward unrestricted fundraising immediately.

Figure 41. Statement of Activities

Domestic Violence Intervention & Prevention Agency
Statement of Activities
For the Six Months Ending December 31, 2005

	Unrestricted	Temporarily Restricted	Permanently Restricted	Total
Contributions	31,477	–	194,500	225,977
Fundraising events	80,269	–	–	80,269
Cost of fundraising events	(17,854)	–	–	(17,854)
Foundation grants	45,000	955,000	70,000	1,070,000
Total support	138,892	955,000	264,500	1,358,392
Government contracts	460,887	–	–	460,887
Interest and dividends	8,754	–	–	8,754
Unrealized gain (loss) on investments	2,251	–	–	2,251
Total revenue	471,892	–	–	471,892
Net assets released from restriction	220,020	(220,020)		–
Total income	830,804	734,980	264,500	1,830,284
Shelter Services	398,547	–	–	398,547
Support Groups	194,012	–	–	194,012
Administration	98,754	–	–	98,754
Fundraising	135,214	–	–	135,214
Total expenses	826,527	–	–	826,527
Change in net assets	4,277	734,980	264,500	1,003,757
Beginning net assets	298,547	371,004	105,000	774,551
Ending net assets	302,824	1,105,984	369,500	1,778,308

Overhead ratio:

$$\frac{\$98,754 + \$135,214}{\$826,527}$$

= 28.31% (28% of every dollar spent goes to DV's overhead costs)

Fundraising return ratio:

$$\frac{\$1,358,392}{\$135,214}$$

= $10.05 (for every $1 spent on fundraising, $10.05 was raised)

Unrestricted fundraising return ratio:

$$\frac{\$138,892}{\$135,214}$$

= 1.03 (for every dollar spent on fundraising, $.03 of unrestricted support was raised)

Funders

Thus far we have looked at the kinds of reporting that staff and board members need in order to monitor and react to changing financial data. Funders, on the other hand, typically require reports during or at the conclusion of their funding of a particular activity. Their interests are focused on the use of their funds and the accomplishments of the program in which they chose to invest. Of course, not all funders are alike. In DV's state contract for shelter services (a fee-for-service contract), DV sends the government agency an invoice each month reflecting the services it provided and the previously negotiated cost per unit of service. Figure 42, Government Contract Invoice, page 103, shows the report DV submits to the state.

Figure 42. Government Contract Invoice

Domestic Violence Intervention & Prevention Agency
Government Contract Invoice
For the Six Months Ending December 31, 2005

	Budget	This Month	YTD	Remaining $	Remaining %	
Shelter Nights						
Single women	2,190	215	1,484	706	32%	
Women with children	4,380	458	1,964	2,416	55%	
Infants/Toddlers	1,095	125	458	637	58%	
Children (2–12)	1,460	158	1,078	382	26%	
Teens (13–18)	730	98	589	141	19%	
Total Number of Nights ❶	9,855	1,054	5,573	4,282	43%	
Reimbursement per night ❷	$82.70	$82.70	$82.70	n/a	n/a	
Total reimbursement due	815,009	87,166	460,887	354,121	43%	

❶ In this fee-for-service contract invoice, DV reports the number of shelter nights (units of service).

❷ And the previously negotiated cost per unit of service.

Foundation funding requires different reporting than government funding. Ideally you want to use a reporting format that demonstrates the full cost of executing a given program as well as the contributions made by the funder in question, other funders, and the organization itself. Figure 43, on page 104, is DV's foundation report. If DV submits this report to the Allen Foundation for instance, not only will the foundation see clearly how its funds were used, but it will also learn what other resources were brought to bear to execute DV's support groups. Even if this much information is not required by a foundation, providing it demonstrates the quality of your tracking systems—both financial and programmatic—and positions you well for future increases in your asking. In short, never give a funder the impression that they are the sole funder of something if they are not.

It may be that a foundation wants to see "its" portion of a program's expenses. In this case, we still recommend that you show the entire program expenditures as in Figure 44, page 105. In this presentation, the Belle Foundation can see the full expenses of the support groups program as well a portion of these expenses assigned to it.

Figure 43. Support Group Program with Funding Sources

Domestic Violence Intervention & Prevention Agency
Support Group Program with Funding Sources
For the Six Months Ending December 31, 2005

	Budget	This Month	YTD	Remaining $	Remaining %
Allen Foundation	160,000	13,458	82,147	77,853	49%
Belle Foundation	180,000	9,875	78,541	101,459	56%
Fong Family Fund	55,000	6,587	21,748	33,252	60%
Greystone Foundation	35,000	5,147	35,000	-	0%
Rhone Rangers Fund	15,000	2,584	2,584	12,416	83%
Agency Contribution	4,114	419	2,000	2,114	51%
Total income	449,114	38,070	222,020	227,094	51%
Salaries	222,028	18,502	106,573	115,455	52%
Payroll taxes	22,758	1,896	11,834	10,924	48%
Employee benefits	24,825	2,069	13,406	11,419	46%
Training	810	–	524	286	35%
Personnel expenses	270,421	22,467	132,337	138,084	51%
Building expenses	8,525	710	4,411	4,114	48%
Conferences and meetings	10,620	125	8,754	1,866	18%
Depreciation	12,058	1,004	5,707	6,351	53%
Dues and subscriptions	2,300	217	1,154	1,146	50%
Equipment rental/maintenance	992	83	536	456	46%
Insurance	8,990	749	3,776	5,214	58%
Interest	2,485	207	1,044	1,441	58%
Other professional fees	13,550	2,575	5,874	7,676	57%
Postage and delivery	2,480	207	1,513	967	39%
Printing and copying	5,000	471	2,578	2,422	48%
Supplies	17,440	1,453	8,574	8,866	51%
Telephone ❶	11,160	930	4,655	6,505	58%
Travel	15,000	1,250	5,834	9,166	61%
Utilities	13,175	1,098	7,265	5,910	45%
Non-personnel expenses	123,775	11,079	61,675	62,100	50%
Total Direct Expenses	394,196	33,546	194,012	200,184	51%
Indirect Costs ❷	54,918	4,577	28,008	26,910	49%
Total Costs	449,114	38,123	222,020	227,094	51%
English Language Groups	360	32	187	173	48%
Spanish Language Groups	100	10	62	38	38%
Chinese Language Groups	36	5	12	24	67%
Total Number of Groups	496	47	261	235	47%
Average cost per group ❸	$905	$811	$851		

❶ For communication with funders, common costs are shown as line items rather than allocated below the line from a common cost pool.

❷ DV is recovering its administrative costs in the Indirect Cost (this is funder terminology) line item.

❸ Including this calculation on reports to funders adds meaning to the financial reports and demonstrates your attention to cost-effective accomplishment of your mission.

Figure 44.   Report to the Belle Foundation

Domestic Violence Intervention & Prevention Agency
Report to the Belle Foundation
For the Six Months Ending December 31, 2005

	Support Groups		Belle Foundation			
	Budget $	YTD $	Budget $	YTD $	Remaining $	%
Salaries	222,028	106,573	95,000	43,875	51,125	54%
Payroll taxes	22,758	11,834	9,500	4,388	5,112	54%
Employee benefits	24,825	13,406	10,450	4,826	5,624	54%
Training	810	524	572	524	48	8%
Personnel expenses	270,421	132,337	115,522	53,613	61,909	54%
Building expenses	8,525	4,411	5,000	1,462	3,538	71%
Conferences and meetings	10,620	8,754	7,500	3,064	4,436	59%
Depreciation	12,058	5,707	–	–	–	
Dues and subscriptions	2,300	1,154	500	439	61	12%
Equipment rental/maintenance	992	536	500	187	313	63%
Insurance	8,990	3,776	–	–	–	
Interest	2,485	1,044	–	–	–	
Other professional fees	13,550	5,874	500	500	–	0%
Postage and delivery	2,480	1,513	1,500	530	970	65%
Printing and copying	5,000	2,578	5,000	902	4,098	82%
Supplies	17,440	8,574	10,000	3,157	6,843	68%
Telephone	11,160	4,655	5,000	1,887	3,113	62%
Travel	15,000	5,834	3,000	2,056	944	31%
Utilities	13,175	7,265	2,500	500	2,000	80%
Non-personnel expenses	123,775	61,675	41,000	14,684	26,316	64%
Total Direct Expenses	394,196	194,012	156,522	68,297	88,225	56%
Indirect Costs	54,918	28,008	23,478	10,244	13,234	56%
Total Costs	449,114	222,020	180,000	78,541	101,459	56%
English Language Groups	360	187	180	94	86	
Spanish Language Groups	100	62	10	6	4	
Chinese Language Groups	36	12	–	–	–	
Total Number of Groups	496	261	190	100	90	
Average cost per group	$905.47	$850.65	$947.37	$785.41		

① This presentation shows the full costs of the Support Group Program, not only the portion covered by the foundation grant.

Constituents

An annual report, including a financial summary, to your broader community sends a clear message of accountability and is also an excellent marketing tool. It is the organization's opportunity to brag about its programmatic accomplishments and demonstrate its financial sustainability. This does not have to be an expensive proposition. While large nonprofits may spend thousands of dollars each year on their annual reports to the community, small groups can self-publish a two- to three-page document or even limit it to a web site version. As the leader, you want this audience to appreciate the financial health of your organization and understand how you used earned and donated resources to accomplish its mission over the past year. Figure 45, Annual Financial Report, is the financial portion of DV's annual report for 2005–06.

The year-end annual financial report is a condensed version of DV's Statement of Activities and its Statement of Financial Position. The presentation gives the reader key information about DV, including its surplus in 2005–06 and its reserve—both signs of strength.

It is a good idea to use simple graphics like pie charts to communicate with the broader community. The most common annual report pie chart is one that shows the reader how resources are allocated across core programs and activities, like the one in Figure 46. With a quick glance, readers of DV's annual report can see that DV directs half of its resources to providing shelter to survivors of domestic violence.

IRS and regulators

As a 501(c)3 nonprofit organization, you are required to submit to the Internal Revenue Service an annual tax return called the Form 990. You can download the form at www.irs.gov. The return is essentially a set of much enhanced financial statements. Following the practices outlined in this book will ensure that your organization can accurately answer the financial questions posed on the form. Not only does the form require key numbers from your Statement of Activities and Statement of Financial Position, but it also inquires about your functional expense totals, your key programmatic accomplishments for the year and how much each cost, the compensation of your key employees and consultants, among other issues. Figure 47, Form 990's Key Financial Questions, page 108, includes some of the key financial questions Form 990 poses and the corresponding DV financial reports where this data is presented.

As the leader, you want constituents to appreciate the financial health of your organization and understand how you used earned and donated resources to accomplish your mission over the past year.

Figure 45. Annual Financial Report

Domestic Violence Intervention & Prevention Agency
Annual Financial Report
For the Year Ending June 30, 2006

Contributions	281,972
Fundraising events - net	148,745
Foundation grants	1,070,000
Government contracts	814,587
Investment income	68,098
Gifts restricted to Endowment	(264,500)
Gifts restricted to Future Years	(425,000)
Total income	1,693,902
Shelter Services	801,882
Support Groups	411,725
Administration	205,334
Fundraising	234,702
Total expenses	1,653,643
Operating Surplus	40,259
Beginning Reserves	272,514
Ending Reserves	312,773

Assets

Cash and Investments	702,342
Contracts and grants receivable	849,759
Property and equipment (net)	157,922
Total assets	1,710,023

Liabilities and Net Assets

Short-term liabilities	88,451
Note payable (net)	89,527
Total liabilities	177,978
Unrestricted net assets	312,773
Temporarily restricted net assets	849,772
Permanently restricted net assets	369,500
Total net assets	1,532,045
Total liabilities and net assets	1,710,023

Figure 46. Annual Financial Report

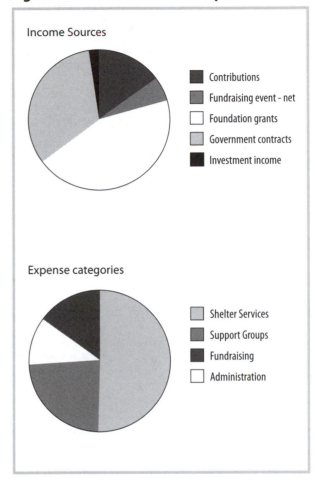

Income Sources

- Contributions
- Fundraising event - net
- Foundation grants
- Government contracts
- Investment income

Expense categories

- Shelter Services
- Support Groups
- Fundraising
- Administration

Figure 47. Form 990's Key Financial Questions

Form 990 Inquiry	Year-end Financial Report with This Data	Sample in This Book
Income sub-totals by type, for example, contributed, earned, special events, and sale of goods	Statement of Activities	Figure 12, page 42
Functional expense totals	Statement of Functional Income and Expenses	Figure 13, page 46
Key program accomplishments and corresponding expense totals	Program Expense Report	Figure 36, page 95
Assets, liabilities, and net assets	Statement of Financial Position	Figure 11, page 39
Compensation for: • Executive director • 5 highest paid staff making $50,000 or more	Annual Staffing Plan	Figure 23, page 72

Form 990 is required of virtually all nonprofits, and because it includes such detailed information, it has become a central component of the nonprofit accountability efforts of the last five plus years. This is manifest in the success of the web site www.guidestar.org, which, through a relationship with the IRS, is scanning hundreds of thousands of Form 990s into a free, searchable database. Form 990 is by law a public document; therefore GuideStar does not need an organization's permission to do this. Executives should visit the GuideStar web site to see if a record of their organization has been created. While you cannot adjust the Form 990s that have been scanned, GuideStar does allow nonprofits to add information about mission and services to their record. State attorneys general also have an interest in Form 990. They are charged with protecting state citizens from solicitation fraud among other things, and most require an annual filing of Form 990. Finally, because it is a public document, you are required to make it available to anyone who asks for it, including your own staff, donors, and the media.

With all of this public access to your Form 990, you should treat it as another communication tool with your key stakeholders. As such, organizational leadership should ensure that the form is completed accurately and on time. We recommend that organizations that have web sites create a PDF of their Form 990s and post them on the site. This demonstrates accountability and allows you to direct inquirers to the site rather than hand copying and mailing requested documents.

Evaluate Your Communication of Financial Progress

Take the organizational evaluation in Figure 48 on page 110 to consider the current quality of communication about financial progress at your nonprofit. Elena's answers and comments are highlighted for your reference under "comments." A complete blank version of the evaluation tool is available in Appendix B.

Summary

Nonprofit leaders who go beyond assessment and budgeting to year-round communication about the organization's financial progress with staff, board, and key stakeholders are at an enormous advantage over their peers who do not. Though it takes more time and means answering more questions, this approach creates buy-in from staff and board and serves to develop them professionally; it ensures their assistance in responding to unanticipated financial challenges or opportunities; and it demonstrates a transparency that sustains people's faith in the organization and its leadership. This last advantage has important ripple effects—from improved staff retention to the increased confidence of your funders.

Figure 48.   Financial Monitoring Assessment

Category	Red	Yellow	Green	Comments	Action Plan
Reporting by Audience	Financial reporting is not tailored to audience.	There is some progress in developing financial reporting for key audiences.	Each key audience is getting the reports it needs according to responsibilities and interests.	We are providing reports to each audience, and we still need to support folks in using and understanding them.	Schedule one-on-one training with each manager.
Financial Indicators	The organization has not selected key financial indicators to monitor.	The organization is learning about ratios and indicators to enable monitoring.	The organization has selected key indicators for review and discussion each month or quarter.	Our indicators are very new; we still need to verify that we have chosen the right ones.	Review and revise indicators as needed.
Reports to Funders	Reports to funders are often late and/or inaccurate.	Reports to funders are produced on time and accurately, according to funder instructions.	Reports to funders are accurate, timely, and as reflective as possible of the full costs of executing activities.	We have not yet communicated the full costs of our programs to our key funders.	Schedule appointments with key funders.
Annual Report	The organization does not do an annual report to the community.	The organization's report to the community lacks clear financial data.	The organization's annual report shares both pro-grammatic successes and meaningful financial data with the community.	To date, our annual report has not included financial data.	Develop a template for integrating financial data into the annual report.
Form 990	Form 990 is late and/or inaccurate.	Form 990 is assumed accurate because it is completed by the auditor each year.	Staff and board review Form 990 before submission each year to ensure accuracy of language and numbers.	We have not paid much attention to Form 990.	Finance committee to review and approve Form 990 before submission.

Conclusion

Few nonprofit executives were drawn to their work by a love of financial assessment, planning, or communication. For most, these are acquired skills and acquired tastes. As trainers and consultants, we have seen the difference a financial leader can make in the health and impact of a nonprofit organization over time. Indeed the most dangerous thing a nonprofit executive can do is to put his or her head in the sand about money. In our experience, relying completely on a bookkeeper or board treasurer simply does not work. It is not an exaggeration to say that the very healthy nonprofits with which we have worked all have executives who view themselves as the financial leaders of their organizations.

Changing an organization's financial culture and systems is almost always a multiyear process. For instance, improving the way your organization does financial planning and budgeting will happen over several budget cycles (years) while staff and board become oriented to what it takes to approach the process inclusively and strategically. Similarly, reaching the quality of financial reporting that is suggested in this book may take a year or more when you consider any necessary staffing/board changes or training, system redesign, and the conceptual work of identifying core programs and activities that need to be tracked and analyzed. In short, if you have a lot to do to improve the financial practices of your nonprofit organization, don't expect it to happen in one quarter or even one fiscal year. Instead, talk with your key staff and board partners about what your priorities are (based on your Red/Yellow/Green Evaluation answers), who will work on them, and what a realistic timeline is.

We hope that this book has offered you a framework in which to consider your personal strengths and weaknesses in this arena, as well as those of your organization. Hopefully, Elena's answers to each chapter evaluation have inspired you to set some personal and organizational goals for the coming year. We believe improvement of financial leadership is an ongoing process. Wherever you are in the process, we congratulate you for making financial leadership a priority, and wish you success in optimizing the financial and programmatic health of the nonprofit business you lead.

It is not an exaggeration to say that the very healthy nonprofits with which we have worked all have executives who view themselves as the financial leaders of their organizations.

Appendix A: Key Terms

A-133

See OMB A-133

Accounts payable

An organization's unpaid bills.

Accounts receivable

Income already promised or earned but not yet received by an organization. Can be further specified, for example, grants receivable, contracts receivable, pledges receivable.

Accrual

The recognition and recording of income when earned and expenses when incurred.

Activity

A core element of the nonprofit organization, for example, key programs, administration, and fundraising. See also allocation, common costs, specific activity costs.

Activity by funding source report

A report that shows how costs for a particular activity are covered by multiple funding sources.

Administrative activity

The finance, legal, board-related, and general oversight of a nonprofit organization.

Allocation

The process of spreading costs to two or more activities. See also activity, allocation basis.

Allocation basis

The rationale for allocation percentages, for example, number of full-time-equivalents (FTE) per activity or total costs before allocation. See also allocation.

Assets

The properties or resources the agency owns and uses, for example, cash, investments, receivables, and equipment. Assets are found on the Statement of Financial Position. See also liquidity.

Audit

The process completed by an auditor that results in an issued opinion on whether year-end financial statements reflect the actual financial activity and condition of the organization for the time period in question.

Below-the-line allocation

The process of allocating total common costs proportionately among the activities of the organization. See also common costs and allocation.

Budget

The organization's plan expressed in dollars (income and expense). Allows the organization to track actual performance against an approved plan.

Budget manager

The staff or board person responsible for collecting information for the budget and building the drafts for staff/board review.

Capitalization

The recording of an item as an asset rather than as an expense when it is purchased. See also depreciation.

Cash basis of accounting

The recognition and recording of income and expenses only when the cash (income) is actually received and the bills are actually paid (expense).

Cash flow

The timing of cash receipts and disbursements.

Chart of accounts

The numerical system for tracking assets, liabilities, net assets, income, and expenses in an accounting system. Drives the reporting capacity of an organization.

Common costs

Those costs that benefit more than one activity and that are not easily identifiable with a single activity. See also activity.

Contingency budget

A budget created to anticipate a potential change to the organization's primary budget, for example, the development of a second budget to be considered if a large grant comes in half-way through a fiscal year.

Contracts receivable

See accounts receivable.

Current assets

Those assets that are cash or can be converted to cash within one year.

Current liabilities

Those liabilities that will be paid within one year.

Current ratio

A comparison of an organization's current assets to its current liabilities; indicates the ability to pay bills and meet financial obligations. See also current assets and current liabilities.

Deficit

Expenses in excess of related income.

Depreciation

The process whereby the cost of a capitalized item is allocated across the years of its useful life. See also capitalization.

Depreciation schedule

A spreadsheet for tracking the purchase of capitalized items and their depreciation status.

Diversification

In reference to nonprofit income, this means having a variety of funding types and sources so that an organization is not unduly dependent on a handful of sources.

Earned revenue

Income that the organization obtains through exchange transactions such as fees, ticket sales, and certain but not all government contracts.

Endowment

A fund permanently restricted by the donor. Interest generated may be unrestricted, temporarily restricted, or permanently restricted.

Fiscal year

The organization's business year, that is, January through December or July through June.

Fixed assets

Assets with a prolonged useful life such as equipment, land, and buildings.

Form 990

The Federal tax return required to be filed annually by most nonprofits.

Full-time equivalent (FTE)

The number of full-time positions at an organization, for example, two full-time staff people and two half-time staff people equals a total of four employees, but three FTE.

Functional expense classification

The presentation of expenses by function: program, administration, and fundraising.

Grants receivable

See accounts receivable.

Internal controls

A set of policies and procedures to prevent deliberate or misguided use of funds for unauthorized purposes.

Liabilities

The debts of the organization, for example, accounts payable, unpaid employee salaries and vacation leave, and loans.

Line of credit

A means of short-term borrowing from a bank to meet cash flow challenges. Should be used for income timing problems, not for profitability problems.

Liquidity

Refers to having assets that are cash or quickly convertible to cash.
See also assets.

Liquid operating reserve

Unrestricted money that the organization has accumulated over time beyond what it needs to pay its immediate bills and other commitments.

Matching principle

Presenting related income and expenses together in the appropriate period. A benefit of accrual basis accounting.

Net assets

The resources ultimately available to the organization (Assets – Liabilities = Net Assets). Found on the Statement of Financial Position. See also reserve.

OMB A-133

The principles for complying with federal contract awards. The A-133 audit is required of all nonprofits that spend more than $500,000 in federal awards in a year.

Output/outcome

These are evaluation concepts. Outputs are the direct results of your efforts (e.g., shelter nights), while outcomes are the longer-term impacts (e.g., injury/deaths of battered spouses avoided).

Overhead activity

The combination of administrative and fundraising activities.

Overhead rate

The percentage calculated by comparing total overhead expenses (administration plus fundraising) to total expenses.

Permanently restricted contributions

Contributions whose principle is to be invested indefinitely according to the donor's wishes.

Program activity

The mission-related work of a nonprofit organization that is not administration or fundraising activity.

Projection

An updated forecast of income and expense.

Ratio

The comparison of two numbers to create a financial indicator. See also current ratio.

Releasing funds from restriction

Spending temporarily restricted funds in accordance with an approved work plan/budget and/or in a specified time frame.

Reserve

The accumulated unrestricted net assets available for the organization's use. See also net assets.

Segments

The unique elements of a chart of accounts. See also chart of accounts.

Specific activity costs

Costs that can be directly associated with a single activity. See also activity.

Statement of activities

Also known as the income statement or profit and loss statement in the for-profit world, this statement reports the financial activity of the organization by function over a period of time.

Statement of financial position

Also known as the balance sheet in the for-profit world, this statement summarizes the assets, liabilities, and net assets of the organization as of a specific date.

Statement of functional income and expense

This report matches income and expense by function, for example, key programs, administration, and fundraising. Used to evaluate surplus/deficit status of each activity.

Temporarily restricted contributions

Grants and contributions that are to be spent for a specific purpose or during a restricted period of time.

Unrealized gains/losses on investments

The amount by which the market value of an asset exceeds or is less than the original cost of that asset.

Unrestricted contributions

Grants and contributions given by the donor without reference to a specific purpose or use within a specific time period.

Variance

Difference between planned and actual financial performance.

Appendix B:
Red/Yellow/Green Evaluation Forms

We have created an evaluation tool that will help you determine where your organization is relative to each component of financial leadership covered in this book.

To use this tool, you will score each measured attribute as being red, yellow, or green. The "red" items are below standard and require immediate attention; "yellow" items are widely practiced though not generally ideal; and "green" items are considered best practice. For more information about this tool, see page 4 and the sample evaluations at the end of each chapter.

Feel free to photocopy the following pages for your own use. Or you can download an electronic copy from the following URLs:

http://www.FieldstoneAlliance.org/worksheets (Code: W44XfL05)

http://www.compasspoint.org

These materials are intended for use in the same way as photocopies, but they are in a form that allows you to type in your responses and reformat the material. Please do not download the material unless you or your organization has purchased this book.

Financial Leadership Assessment (BLANK)

This form accompanies Chapter 1.

Category	Getting Started	A Work in Progress	Key Competency	Comments	Action Plan
Personal Leadership	I do not yet consider myself the financial leader of this organization.	I am trying to consider myself the financial leader of this organization.	I absolutely consider myself the financial leader of this organization.		
Priorities	The financial health of this organization is not yet one of my top priorities.	The financial health of this organization is becoming one of my top priorities.	The financial health of this organization is absolutely one of my top priorities.		
Information Sharing	I do not yet share financial information with staff, and I regularly raise both programmatic and financial issues for consideration at our meetings.	I am working on sharing financial information with staff, and I regularly raise both programmatic and financial issues for consideration at our meetings.	I absolutely share financial information with staff, and I regularly raise both programmatic and financial issues for consideration at our meetings.		
Board of Directors	I do not yet ensure that my board of directors discusses our financial situation at every board meeting.	I am working toward ensuring that my board of directors discusses our financial situation at every board meeting.	I ensure that my board of directors discusses our financial situation at every board meeting.		
Teamwork	I have not yet surrounded myself with enough financially savvy staff, consultants, and board members to feel confident that we have the necessary financial guidance for our organization.	I am trying to surround myself with enough financially savvy staff, consultants, and board members to feel confident that we have the necessary financial guidance for our organization.	I absolutely have surrounded myself with enough financially savvy staff, consultants, and board members to feel confident that we have the necessary financial guidance for our organization.		

Financial Leadership Assessment continued

Category	Getting Started	A Work in Progress	Key Competency	Comments	Action Plan
Financial Knowledge	Without consulting financial statements or budgets, I cannot yet readily name our core programs and offer a good estimate of how much we'll spend on each this year.	Without consulting financial statements or budgets, I can almost name our core programs and offer a good estimate of how much we'll spend on each this year.	Without consulting financial statements or budgets, I can readily name our core programs and offer a good estimate of how much we'll spend on each this year.		
Financial Performance	I do not yet know which of our core activities generate surpluses and which lose money.	I almost have a handle on which of our core activities generate surpluses and which lose money.	I absolutely know which of our core activities generate surpluses and which lose money.		
Investment in Infrastructure	I do not yet feel as comfortable investing the organization's resources in a great bookkeeper as I do in a great program staff person.	I feel almost as comfortable investing the organization's resources in a great bookkeeper as I do in a great program staff person.	I absolutely feel as comfortable investing the organization's resources in a great bookkeeper as I do in a great program staff person.		
Funder Accountability	I am not yet ready to share our financial data with our funders and stakeholders.	I am almost ready to help our funders and stakeholders understand how we use financial resources to accomplish our mission.	I absolutely want our funders and stakeholders to understand how we use financial resources to accomplish our mission.		
Establish a Culture of Transparency around Money	The staff and board do not yet know for sure that I value financial transparency.	The staff and board are beginning to understand that I value financial transparency.	The staff and board absolutely know for sure that I value financial transparency.		

Accurate Financial Data Assessment (BLANK)

This form accompanies Chapter 2.

Category	Red	Yellow	Green	Comments	Action Plan
Accounting Software	The accounting software is inadequate for the organization's tracking and reporting needs.	The accounting software is adequate for the organization's tracking and reporting needs, but not well implemented.	The accounting software is adequate for the organization's tracking and reporting needs and has been implemented to support optimal financial reporting.		
Staffing	The providers of financial reports to management and board are not trained in the specifics of nonprofit accounting.	The providers of financial reports to management and board are in the process of being trained in the specifics of nonprofit accounting.	The providers of financial reports to management and board are well trained in the specifics of nonprofit accounting.		
Accounting Practices	None of the five key accounting practices are being followed.	Most of the five key accounting practices are being followed.	Each of the five key accounting practices is being followed.		

Accurate Financial Data Assessment continued

Category	Red	Yellow	Green	Comments	Action Plan
Internal Controls	Internal controls are not in place.	Some controls are in place but leadership has not prioritized optimal internal controls.	Because of leadership's emphasis on accountability and transparency, internal controls are prioritized and ensured.		
Chart of Accounts	The chart of accounts is managed solely by the bookkeeper and does not reflect the current activities of the organization.	The chart of accounts is fairly reflective of current activities, but needs updating.	The chart of accounts is reviewed and understood by key staff and board. It reflects current activities.		
Financial Reporting	The content of the monthly financial package varies and may consist of a simple overall income and expense report.	The monthly financial package includes (at least) a Statement of Activities and a Statement of Position.	The monthly financial package includes a Statement of Position, a Budgeted Statement of Activities, a Statement of Functional Income and Expense, and an updated Cash Flow Forecast.		

Financial Health Assessment (BLANK)
This form accompanies Chapter 3.

Category	Red	Yellow	Green	Comments	Action Plan
Current Ratio	Ratio of current assets to current liabilities is less than 1:1.	Ratio of current assets to current liabilities is between 1:1 and 3:1.	Ratio of current assets to current liabilities is greater than 3:1.		
Cash Flow	Cash flow is a constant problem resulting in frequent delays in payroll and late fees from vendors.	We have occasional periods of cash flow challenge, which we weather by delaying select payments to vendors.	Cash flow is either not a challenge or the challenge is anticipated and managed by delaying large expenditures or use of a line of credit.		
Budget Variances	The organization has large variances between planned and actual income for the year to date, but continues to spend at the pace originally budgeted.	While there are some variances between planned and actual income for the year to date, we have reduced spending to maintain our planned year-end surplus/deficit.	We are on track with our financial plan for the year.		
Cash Management	The finance manager leaves all idle cash in the operating checking account.	The finance manager moves idle cash to an interest-bearing account.	At the direction of the board finance committee, the finance manager pursues investment opportunities in line with the organization's documented Investment Policy.		
Restricted Fund Balance	The organization has less cash and receivables than its total restricted net assets.	The organization has as much cash and receivables as it has total restricted net assets.	The organization has more cash and receivables than its total restricted net assets.		
Releases from Restriction	The organization does not budget for or routinely assess its release of funds from restriction.	The organization is behind its plan for the year in releasing funds from restriction.	The organization is meeting its goal for the year of releasing funds from restriction.		

Financial Health Assessment continued

Category	Red	Yellow	Green	Comments	Action Plan
Overhead Rate	The organization has an overhead rate of less than 15% or more than 30%.	The organization has an overhead rate between 26% and 30%.	The organization has an overhead rate of between 15% and 25%.		
Fundraising Effectiveness	The organization has no targets for fundraising return and never calculates it.	The organization maintains some fundraising efforts that are not cost-effective.	The organization ensures the cost-effectiveness of its fundraising efforts.		
Cost per Unit	The organization has no targets for cost per unit and does not monitor it.	The organization has a cost per unit that is not competitive with other organizations doing similar work.	The organization has a cost per unit that is competitive with other organizations doing similar work.		
Operating Reserve	The organization has an unrestricted reserve of less than one month's operating expenses.	The organization has an unrestricted reserve of between one and three month's operating expenses.	The organization has an unrestricted reserve of four to twelve month's operating expenses.		
Profit/Loss by Activity	The organization does not have financial data by activity, so it cannot determine how core programs are performing financially.	The organization is carrying multiple programs with significant operating deficits.	While some core programs run small deficits, management focuses on recovering all possible costs from key funders and raising unrestricted support for subsidization.		
Program Portfolio	Leadership does not assess the sustainability of our mix of activities.	Based upon recent assessment, leadership is trying to shift the mission-impact and/or financial sustainability of some core activities.	The organization has a good portfolio of activities that together result in high mission impact and financial health.		
Diversity of Funding	The organization is dependent on a handful of funding sources of a single type.	The organization relies on multiple funding sources across two types of funding.	The organization relies on many sources across three or more funding streams.		

Financial Planning Assessment (BLANK)

This form accompanies Chapter 4.

Category	Red	Yellow	Green	Comments	Action Plan
Budget Process	We have no annual budget	The annual budget is not a true reflection of our work plan for the year.	The annual budget is our planning and monitoring tool.		
Participation	The finance manager and/or executive director creates the budget.	The finance manager and/or executive director creates the budget with some input from other managers.	The budgeting process is inclusive and demands that all activity managers engage in meaningful planning for the year to come.		
Expense Forecasting	We estimate costs based solely on our known grants and contracts.	We estimate our costs based on both what's known in our grants and what it would cost to do the best work possible.	We start by estimating what it would cost to do the best work possible, regardless of who funds it.		
Income Projection	We do no historical analysis and regularly overestimate income for the year.	Based on historical analysis, we generally come close to accurately forecasting income.	Using historical analysis and current data gathering, we forecast income realistically.		
Striking the Balance	Leadership thinks a good budget is a balanced budget.	Leadership strives for a balanced or slight surplus budget.	Leadership considers available resources and current opportunities in deciding whether to build a deficit, balanced, or surplus budget.		
Revision	We "true up" our budget throughout the year to correct for inaccurate planning.	At midyear we consider revising our budget if there are material inaccuracies in the expenses and/or income targets.	While we sometimes have to revise the budget, we use contingency budgeting to prepare board and staff for likely scenarios.		

Financial Monitoring Assessment (BLANK)

This form accompanies Chapter 5.

Category	Red	Yellow	Green	Comments	Action Plan
Reporting by Audience	Financial reporting is not tailored to audience.	There is some progress in developing financial reporting for key audiences.	Each key audience is getting the reports it needs according to responsibilities and interests.		
Financial Indicators	The organization has not selected key financial indicators to monitor.	The organization is learning about ratios and indicators to enable monitoring.	The organization has selected key indicators for review and discussion each month or quarter.		
Reports to Funders	Reports to funders are often late and/or inaccurate.	Reports to funders are produced on time and accurately, according to funder instructions.	Reports to funders are accurate, timely, and as reflective as possible of the full costs of executing activities.		
Annual Report	The organization does not do an annual report to the community.	The organization's report to the community lacks clear financial data.	The organization's annual report shares both programmatic successes and meaningful financial data with the community.		
Form 990	Form 990 is late and/or inaccurate.	Form 990 is assumed accurate because it is completed by the auditor each year.	Staff and board review Form 990 before submission each year to ensure accuracy of language and numbers.		

Appendix C: Resources

Periodicals

Making time for regular review of nonprofit business periodicals is an aspect of financial leadership. The following are national periodicals that we use regularly to stay informed about trends in nonprofit management and philanthropy.

The Chronicle of Philanthropy

This bi-weekly calls itself the "newspaper of the nonprofit world." It has regular articles about philanthropy trends and nonprofit leadership.

The Chronicle of Philanthropy
1255 Twenty-Third Street, N.W.
Washington, DC 20037
800-728-2819
www.philanthropy.com

The NonProfit Times

This newspaper is published twenty-four times per year and calls itself "the leading business publication for nonprofit management." It has regular columns on finances and taxes. Subscriptions are free to nonprofit executives.

The NonProfit Times
120 Littleton Road, Suite 120
Parsippany, NJ 07054-1803
973-394-1800
www.nptimes.com

The Nonprofit Quarterly

This quarterly magazine focuses on nonprofit management trends. It features articles on emerging issues by sector thought-leaders along with regular columns on finance.

The Nonprofit Quarterly
Third Sector New England
18 Tremont Street, Suite 700
Boston, MA 02108
800-281-7770
www.nonprofitquarterly.org

The Stanford Social Innovation Review

The *Stanford Social Innovation Review* is a quarterly publication of the Stanford Graduate School of Business targeted to corporate, nonprofit, and philanthropic leaders.

Stanford Social Innovation Review
518 Memorial Way
Stanford University
Stanford, CA 94305-5016
www.ssireview.com

Books on Nonprofit Finance

These are books that delve deeper into some of the issues addressed in this book. They are resources you may want to provide to your finance staff as part of their professional development.

All the Way to the Bank

LarsonAllen Public Service Group
www.larsonallen.com/publicservice/

This guide focuses on money management and includes chapters on annual auditing and compliance, cash management and investment, and borrowing.

Bookkeeping Basics

Debra L. Ruegg and Lisa M. Venkatrathnam
LarsonAllen Public Service Group
Fieldstone Alliance

This is a practical guide to bookkeeping. It's ideal for the self-taught bookkeeper or the bookkeeper new to the nonprofit world.

990 Handbook: A Line-by-Line Approach

Wiley Nonprofit Series
www.wiley.com/nonprofit

This is a readable guide to understanding and completing IRS Form 990. It is also a good resource for those who outsource completion of Form 990, but want to understand what the form is asking about a nonprofit's finances and operations.

Unified Financial Reporting System for Not-for-Profit Organizations

Jossey-Bass
www.josseybass.com

This guide introduces the Unified Chart of Accounts—a tool to standardize nonprofit reporting and help organizations be responsive in the design of their accounting systems to Form 990 and government contracting standards.

Financial and Accounting Guide for Not-for-Profit Organizations

Wiley Nonprofit Series
www.wiley.com/nonprofit

This very technical resource is updated annually and serves as the definitive guide to nonprofit accounting rules and procedures.

QuickBooks for Not-for-Profit Organizations

Sleeter Group
www.sleeter.com or www.compasspoint.org

This is a step-by-step guide to setting up and using QuickBooks Pro to doing nonprofit accounting.

Accounting Software

As consultants to nonprofit organizations, we do not recommend certain software over others. We believe the focus should be on buying a product that matches your staff capacity and financial complexity. Here is a non-comprehensive list of products (from least expensive upward) that we have noted for their success with community-based nonprofits.

QuickBooks Pro and QuickBooks Premiere for Nonprofits

www.intuit.com

Fund E-Z

www.fundez.com

Cyma Not-for-Profit Edition

www.cyma.com

Micro Information Products (MIP)

www.mip.com

Intuit FundWare

www.fundware.com

Blackbaud Financial Edge

www.blackbaud.com

Accountability Web Sites

www.give.org

This is the web site of the Better Business Bureau/Wise Giving Alliance, which collects and distributes information on hundreds of nonprofit organizations that solicit nationally or have national or international program services. It routinely asks such organizations for information about their programs, governance, fundraising practices, and finances when the charities have been the subject of inquiries.

www.guidestar.org

GuideStar is a searchable database of Form 990s and other information about public charities. All organizations should review and update their GuideStar records periodically. The site also offers specialized search functions.

More results-oriented books from Fieldstone Alliance

Finance

Bookkeeping Basics
What Every Nonprofit Bookkeeper Needs to Know
by Debra L. Ruegg and Lisa M. Venkatrathnam

Complete with step-by-step instructions, a glossary of accounting terms, detailed examples, and handy reproducible forms, this book will enable you to successfully meet the basic bookkeeping requirements of your nonprofit organization—even if you have little or no formal accounting training.

128 pages, softcover   Item # 069296

Coping with Cutbacks
The Nonprofit Guide to Success When Times Are Tight
by Emil Angelica and Vincent Hyman

Shows you practical ways to involve business, government, and other nonprofits to solve problems together. Also includes 185 cutback strategies you can put to use right away.

128 pages, softcover   Item # 069091

Financial Leadership for Nonprofit Executives
Guiding Your Organization to Long-term Success
by Jeanne Peters and Elizabeth Schaffer

Provides executives with a practical guide to protecting and growing the assets of their organizations and with accomplishing as much mission as possible with those resources.

144 pages, softcover   Item # 06944X

Venture Forth! The Essential Guide to Starting a Moneymaking Business in Your Nonprofit Organization
by Rolfe Larson

The most complete guide on nonprofit business development. Building on the experience of dozens of organizations, this handbook gives you a time-tested approach for finding, testing, and launching a successful nonprofit business venture.

272 pages, softcover   Item # 069245

Management & Leadership

The Accidental Techie
Supporting, Managing, and Maximizing Your Nonprofit's Technology
by Sue Bennett, CompassPoint Nonprofit Services

How to support and manage technology on a day-to-day basis including setting up a help desk, developing an effective technology budget and implementation plan, working with consultants, handling viruses, creating a backup system, purchasing hardware and software, using donated hardware, creating a useful database, and more.

176 pages, softcover   Item # 069490

Benchmarking for Nonprofits
How to Measure, Manage, and Improve Results
by Jason Saul

Benchmarking—the onging process of measuring your organization against leaders—can help stimulate innovation, increase your impact, decrease your costs, impress your funders, engage your board, and sharpen your mission. This book defines a formal, systematic, and reliable way to benchmark, from preparing your organization to measuring performance and implementing best practices.

128 pages, softcover   Item # 069431

The Best of the Board Café
Hands-on Solutions for Nonprofit Boards
by Jan Masaoka, CompassPoint Nonprofit Services

Gathers the most requested articles from the e-newsletter, *Board Café*. You'll find a lively menu of ideas, information, opinions, news, and resources to help board members give and get the most out of their board service.

232 pages, softcover   Item # 069407

Consulting with Nonprofits: A Practitioner's Guide
by Carol A. Lukas

A step-by-step, comprehensive guide for consultants. Addresses the art of consulting, how to run your business, and much more. Also includes tips and anecdotes from thirty skilled consultants.

240 pages, softcover   Item # 069172

The Fieldstone Nonprofit Guide to Crafting Effective Mission and Vision Statements
by Emil Angelica

Guides you through two six-step processes that result in a mission statement, vision statement, or both. Shows how a clarified mission and vision lead to more effective leadership, decisions, fundraising, and management. Includes tips, sample statements, and worksheets.

88 pages, softcover   Item # 06927X

The Fieldstone Nonprofit Guide to Developing Effective Teams
by Beth Gilbertsen and Vijit Ramchandani

Helps you understand, start, and maintain a team. Provides tools and techniques for writing a mission statement, setting goals, conducting effective meetings, creating ground rules to manage team dynamics, making decisions in teams, and developing team spirit.

80 pages, softcover   Item # 069202

The Five Life Stages of Nonprofit Organizations
Where You Are, Where You're Going, and What to Expect When You Get There
by Judith Sharken Simon with J. Terence Donovan

Shows you what's "normal" for each development stage which helps you plan for transitions, stay on track, and avoid unnecessary struggles. This guide also includes The Nonprofit Life Stage Assessment to plot and understand your organization's progress in seven arenas of organization development.

128 pages, softcover   Item # 069229

For current prices, a catalog, or to order call 800-274-6024

The Manager's Guide to Program Evaluation:
Planning, Contracting, and Managing for Useful Results
by Paul W. Mattessich, PhD

Explains how to plan and manage an evaluation that will help identify your organization's successes, share information with key audiences, and improve services.

96 pages, softcover   Item # 069385

The Nonprofit Mergers Workbook
The Leader's Guide to Considering, Negotiating, and Executing a Merger
by David La Piana

A merger can be a daunting and complex process. Save time, money, and untold frustration with this highly practical guide that makes the process manageable and controllable.

240 pages, softcover   Item # 069210

The Nonprofit Mergers Workbook Part II
Unifying the Organization after a Merger
by La Piana Associates

Once the merger agreement is signed, the question becomes: How do we make this merger work? *Part II* helps you create a comprehensive plan to achieve *integration*—bringing together people, programs, processes, and systems from two (or more) organizations into a single, unified whole.

248 pages, includes CD-ROM   Item # 069415

Nonprofit Stewardship
A Better Way to Lead Your Mission-Based Organization
by Peter C. Brinckerhoff

You may lead a not-for-profit organization, but it's not your organization. It belongs to the community it serves. You are the steward—the manager of resources that belong to someone else. The stewardship model of leadership can help your organization improve its mission capability by forcing you to keep your organization's mission foremost. It helps you make decisions that are best for the people your organization serves. In other words, stewardship helps you do more good for more people.

272 pages, softcover   Item # 069423

Resolving Conflict in Nonprofit Organizations
The Leader's Guide to Finding Constructive Solutions
by Marion Peters Angelica

Helps you identify conflict, decide whether to intervene, uncover and deal with the true issues, and design and conduct a conflict resolution process. Includes exercises to learn and practice conflict resolution skills, guidance on handling unique conflicts such as harassment and discrimination, and when (and where) to seek outside help with litigation, arbitration, and mediation.

192 pages, softcover   Item # 069164

Strategic Planning Workbook for Nonprofit Organizations, Revised and Updated
by Bryan Barry

Chart a wise course for your nonprofit's future. This time-tested workbook gives you practical step-by-step guidance, real-life examples, one nonprofit's complete strategic plan, and easy-to-use worksheets.

144 pages, softcover   Item # 069075

The Fieldstone Nonprofit Guide to
Conducting Successful Focus Groups
by Judith Sharken Simon

Shows how to collect valuable information without a lot of money or special expertise. Using this proven technique, you'll get essential opinions and feedback to help you check out your assumptions, do better strategic planning, improve services or products, and more.

80 pages, softcover   Item # 069199

Marketing Workbook for Nonprofit Organizations Volume I: Develop the Plan
by Gary J. Stern

Don't just wish for results—get them! Here's how to create a straightforward, usable marketing plan. Includes the six Ps of Marketing, how to use them effectively, a sample marketing plan, tips on using the Internet, and worksheets.

208 pages, softcover   Item # 069253

Marketing Workbook for Nonprofit Organizations Volume II: Mobilize People for Marketing Success
by Gary J. Stern

Put together a successful promotional campaign based on the most persuasive tool of all: personal contact. Learn how to mobilize your entire organization, its staff, volunteers, and supporters in a focused, one-to-one marketing campaign. Comes with *Pocket Guide for Marketing Representatives*. In it, your marketing representatives can record key campaign messages and find motivational reminders.

192 pages, softcover   Item # 069105

Community Building: What Makes It Work
by Wilder Research Center

Reveals twenty-eight keys to help you build community more effectively. Includes detailed descriptions of each factor, case examples of how they play out, and practical questions to assess your work.

112 pages, softcover   Item # 069121

Community Economic Development Handbook
by Mihailo Temali

A concrete, practical handbook to turning any neighborhood around. It explains how to start a community economic development organization, and then lays out the steps of four proven and powerful strategies for revitalizing inner-city neighborhoods.

288 pages, softcover   Item # 069369

The Fieldstone Nonprofit Guide to
Conducting Community Forums
by Carol Lukas and Linda Hoskins

Provides step-by-step instruction to plan and carry out exciting, successful community forums that will educate the public, build consensus, focus action, or influence policy.

128 pages, softcover   Item # 069318

Collaboration

Collaboration Handbook
Creating, Sustaining, and Enjoying the Journey
by Michael Winer and Karen Ray

Shows you how to get a collaboration going, set goals, determine everyone's roles, create an action plan, and evaluate the results. Includes a case study of one collaboration from start to finish, helpful tips on how to avoid pitfalls, and worksheets to keep everyone on track.

192 pages, softcover   Item # 069032

Collaboration: What Makes It Work, 2nd Ed.
by Paul Mattessich, PhD, Marta Murray-Close, BA, and Barbara Monsey, MPH

An in-depth review of current collaboration research. Major findings are summarized, critical conclusions are drawn, and twenty key factors influencing successful collaborations are identified. Includes The Wilder Collaboration Factors Inventory, which groups can use to assess their collaboration.

104 pages, softcover   Item # 069326

A Fieldstone Nonprofit Guide to
Forming Alliances
by Linda Hoskins and Emil Angelica

Helps you understand the wide range of ways that they can work with others—focusing on alliances that work at a lower level of intensity. It shows how to plan and start an alliance that fits a nonprofit's circumstances and needs.

112 pages, softcover   Item # 069466

The Nimble Collaboration
Fine-Tuning Your Collaboration for Lasting Success
by Karen Ray

Shows you ways to make your collaboration more responsive, flexible, and productive. Provides three key strategies to help your collaboration respond quickly to changing environments and participants.

136 pages, softcover   Item # 069288

Lobbying & Advocacy

The Lobbying and Advocacy Handbook
for Nonprofit Organizations
Shaping Public Policy at the State and Local Level
by Marcia Avner

The Lobbying and Advocacy Handbook is a planning guide and resource for nonprofit organizations that want to influence issues that matter to them. This book will help you decide whether to lobby and then put plans in place to make it work.

240 pages, softcover   Item # 069261

The Nonprofit Board Member's Guide to
Lobbying and Advocacy
by Marcia Avner

Written specifically for board members, this guide helps organizations increase their impact on policy decisions. It reveals how board members can be involved in planning for and implementing successful lobbying efforts.

96 pages, softcover   Item # 069393

Board Tools

The Best of the Board Café
Hands-on Solutions for Nonprofit Boards
by Jan Masaoka, CompassPoint Nonprofit Services

Gathers the most requested articles from the e-newsletter, *Board Café*. You'll find a lively menu of ideas, information, opinions, news, and resources to help board members give and get the most out of their board service.

232 pages, softcover   Item # 069407

The Nonprofit Board Member's Guide to
Lobbying and Advocacy
by Marcia Avner
96 pages, softcover   Item # 069393

Funder's Guides

Community Visions, Community Solutions
Grantmaking for Comprehensive Impact
by Joseph A. Connor and Stephanie Kadel-Taras

Helps foundations, community funds, government agencies, and other grantmakers uncover a community's highest aspiration for itself, and support and sustain strategic efforts to get to workable solutions.

128 pages, softcover   Item # 06930X

A Funder's Guide to Evaluation: Leveraging Evaluation to
Improve Nonprofit Effectiveness
by Peter York

More and more funders and nonprofit leaders are shifting away from proving something to someone else, and toward *im*-proving what they do so they can achieve their mission and share how they succeeded with others. This book includes strategies and tools to help grantmakers support and use evaluation as a nonprofit organizational capacity-building tool.

160 pages, softcover   Item # 069482

Strengthening Nonprofit Performance
A Funder's Guide to Capacity Building
by Paul Connolly and Carol Lukas

This practical guide synthesizes the most recent capacity building practice and research into a collection of strategies, steps, and examples that you can use to get started on or improve funding to strengthen nonprofit organizations.

176 pages, softcover   Item # 069377